·b·ırn

Mussolini and Fascism

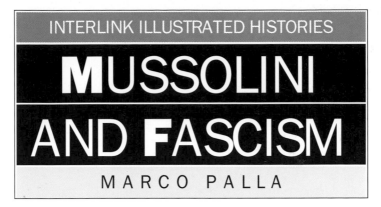

INTERLINK ILLUSTRATED HISTORIES

MUSSOLINI
AND FASCISM

MARCO PALLA

Translated by Arthur Figliola and
Claudia Rattazzi Papka

INTERLINK BOOKS

An imprint of Interlink Publishing Group, Inc.
New York

First American edition published in 2000 by

INTERLINK BOOKS

An imprint of Interlink Publishing Group, Inc.

99 Seventh Avenue · Brooklyn, New York 11215 and
46 Crosby Street · Northampton, Massachusetts 01060

Copyright © Giunti Gruppo Editoriale — Casterman, 1993, 2000
Translation copyright © Interlink Publishing 2000

This edition of *Mussolini and Fascism* is published by arrangement
with Giunti Gruppo Editoriale and Casterman Editions.

Library of Congress Cataloging-in-Publication Data

Palla, Marco.
    [Mussolini e il fascismo. English]
    Mussolini and fascism / Marco Palla ; [Trans. Claudia Rattazzi
Papka].
        p. cm. — (Interlink illustrated histories)
    Includes bibliographical references and index.
    ISBN 1-56656-340-2
    1. Italy—Politics and government—1922–1945. 2. Mussolini,
Benito, 1883–1945. 3. Fascism—Italy. I. Rattazzi Papka, Claudia.
II. Title. III. Series.
DG571.P22613   1999
945.091—dc21   99-44263
                                                 CIP

Typeset by Archetype IT Ltd., website: www.archetype-it.com
Printed and bound in Italy

To order or request our complete catalog,
please call us at **1-800-238-LINK** or write to:
Interlink Publishing
46 Crosby Street, Northampton, MA 01060
e-mail: info@interlinkbooks.com • website: www.interlinkbooks.com

Contents

MUSSOLINI AND FASCISM

Chapter 1

THE **R**ISE
TO **P**OWER

IN THE GENERAL ELECTIONS OF 1919, THE NEW FASCIST MOVEMENT OBTAINED ONLY 4,000 VOTES AND NO ELECTED DEPUTY; THREE YEARS LATER THE FASCISTS MARCHED ON ROME AND THE KING CHARGED MUSSOLINI WITH THE FORMATION OF A NEW GOVERNMENT. WITHIN A FEW MONTHS, THE ITALIAN LIBERAL SYSTEM HAD COLLAPSED, WITHOUT EVEN MAKING TOO MUCH NOISE.

I n the history of the twentieth century, fascism has had a prominent role, reaching far beyond its Italian origins. At the same time, the Italian causes of this historically important phenomenon have complex roots in problems and questions that lie even deeper in Italy's history than the years of the First World War and the 1920s. Precursory conditions have often been traced in the history of the previous century; it is not possible to consider them all here. But it is important to recall the fragility of the Italian political system and its out-of-date economic and social structures to have an idea, although a general and summary one, of the background upon which were grafted, in the years between 1919 and 1922, the most immediate and specific reasons for the rise of fascism and then for its success.

The belated political unification of Italy is certainly among the causes that contribute indirectly to explaining the authoritarian backlash of the period 1922–1943 (just as the late political unification of Germany is among the indirect causes of the rise of Nazism). This political unification was forged between 1859 and 1861, continued with the addition of Venice and the Veneto in 1866, and Rome and Lazio in 1870, and was completed only with the addition of Trent and Trieste in 1918.

Mussolini leads a demonstration of adherents to the Fasci di Combattimento, *the movement founded by him in 1919, through the streets of Milan. It was 1920 and fascism was about to become the most important party ever to have existed in the history of the Kingdom of Italy.*

A foxhunting scene in the Roman countryside, from an 1890 photograph by Giuseppe Primoli, pioneer of Italian photography. The Italian ruling class at the end of the nineteenth century tailored its tastes to those of the other European aristocracies. But on social and economic levels, the Kingdom of Italy was paying the price for belated unification and ancient imbalances.

Even more belated was the process of industrialization and modernization in Italy, which was far from overcoming the enormous weight of the ancient, centuries-old imbalances among the territories and regions, as well as between the city and the countryside. The most obvious examples of these are the Southern question and the limited diffusion (both oral and written) of the national language.

The Failure of the Liberal Oligarchy

The obsession with unification among the ruling class in the years following 1861 gave way to a political and administrative system dominated by the most rigid centralism, and marked by paternalism and inclinations that were moderate yet openly authoritarian. This reduced the democratic left to opposition and definitively blocked the already reluctant and uncertain reforming vocation of Italian liberalism. The monarchist and constitutional State — which however had no constitution of its own, since the one given by Charles Albert to his Kingdom of Sardinia in 1848 had simply

been extended to all of Italy after 1861 — presided over a process of democratization that would hinge on the extension of suffrage and on the central role of parliament.

If immediately after unification only two percent of Italians enjoyed the right to vote, the electoral reforms of the 1880s and the first years of the 1900s modified this blatantly artificial situation only slightly. In the "democracy" of liberal Italy the reforms that brought Italians (though only males) the vote for the first time in 1913, and confirmed and later developed universal suffrage through proportional representation in time for the 1919 elections, gave fresh proof of the consensus gathered by the Catholics and socialists. But these had in different ways been kept on the margins of the liberal political system.

From the nineteenth to the twentieth century, furthermore, Italy faced the loss of several million emigrants, pushed by poverty to the Americas. Nor were any social reforms, particularly agricultural ones, introduced that were able to reverse this tendency. And the

At the end of the last century, a group of emigrants waits on the wharf of the port of Naples to embark for America. Several million Italians, in the last years of the nineteenth and first years of the twentieth century, were drawn to emigrate overseas by the prospect of better economic conditions.

*Giovannni Giolitti strolls at the
seaside in Ostia in 1922, on the
eve of Mussolini's accession to
power. In the years preceding the
Great War, Giolitti had dominated
the Italian political scene, and
with him the oligarchy of the
Kingdom of Italy made its last,
vain attempt to find a
compromise between the spirit of
conservatism and the need for
renewal.
Right, an Italian trench between
the Adige and Lake Garda in the
First World War.*

first colonial enterprises (from the failed attempt on
Ethiopia in 1896 to the conquest of Libya in 1912)
were also far from able to provide for the Italian farmers
those African lands that imperialist propaganda had
never tired of promising them.

The "Giolitti era" (as the period between 1900 and
1914, dominated by the political figure of Giovanni
Giolitti, is generally called) was the relatively brief
period in which the greatest efforts were made to medi-
ate between the push for socio-political reform and the
spirit of conservatism. But the inclusive balance of this
phase has been pointed to by many historians as the
failure of liberalism, a failure that in part explains the
essential causes of the rise of fascism.

In 1915, the dominant oligarchy had the strength to
take Italy, ill-prepared and fragile as it was, into the
Great War, from which the country emerged demographically, economically, and socially weakened and
thus incapable of overcoming an ever-worsening political crisis.

The History of Italy and the History of Fascism

Fascism was the particular solution to this Italian crisis: a break with the ambiguous, belated, and fragile

In 1915, the dominant oligarchy had the strength to take Italy, ill-prepared and fragile, into the Great War, from which the country emerged demographically, economically, and socially weakened and thus incapable of overcoming an ever-worsening political crisis.

process of democratization. It was a solution that discounted many elements of continuity with the recent past, and yet it was precisely from such archaic and authoritarian vestiges that, in various ways, it was inspired. Nevertheless, fascism was a modern reaction, which did not limit itself to the restoration of the old order. Its characteristics will be illustrated in the following pages.

This work is not, however, and does not wish to be a history of Italy in the fascist period, which is a broader and more complex topic than that definable only as the history of fascism. I have tried, naturally, to map the character and the nature, the function and the scope of the fascist phenomenon from the point of view of its historical impact on Italy, and not only on Italy, between the two World Wars. But it is always wise to remember, as a methodological caveat, that it is not correct to attribute to fascism, for good or bad, all that happened in Italy during those years: in the economy; in the social

Mussolini in 1919, together with the founders of the Fasci di Combattimento, *the new movement to which the former socialist hitched his political fortunes in the post-war years.*

hierarchy; in demographic evolution; in literature and cinema, architecture and poetry, science and philosophy; in fashion; in public and private mentalities; in daily life; in education; in leisure time....

Just as fascism and the figure of Mussolini are inseparable, but are not the same thing, so the parabola of fascism and the history of Italy — the history of Italian society, of Italian men and women — from 1919 to 1945 can neither be separated nor considered identical.

Mussolini from Socialism to Fascism

From the modern era until today the Italian language has given many words to the global lexicon of theater and music. But the term "fascism" is perhaps the only Italian word that has been universally diffused in the contemporary political lexicon.

The use of this word has certainly broadened to include in our day the most diverse examples of authoritarian movements and groups, oriented to the right and endorsing violence, in areas and continents far from Italy and Europe. "Fascist" has also often become synonymous with an injurious epithet wielded against oppressors of any type. The idea of fascism, then, is contradictory, changeable and confused, mutable by means of disguises and transformations; it is a neologism that can only with great difficulty be interpreted with an unambiguous or definitive classification.

To return the term to its genuine historical context it is again necessary to take into account the fact just alluded to, which underlines the enduring ambiguity of the word. Unlike words such as "conservatism" or "socialism," and also "radicalism" or "democracy" (and all the different meanings accorded to this last term), in the name fascism there is no specific message. The word derives from *fascio* (literally a bundle or bunch), a union of forces that can be of diverse origin or formation. But union to what end? The monotonous rhetoric of "Latin" superiority, which the fascist regime spouted unrelentingly in the course of the 1930s, should not fool us with its harking back to the lictors' fasces that symbolized political authority in ancient republican

Mussolini at 30, in 1914, when he was still heading the socialist newspaper Avanti!. In face of the question of Italy's intervention in the war, however, Mussolini's repudiation of his internationalist and socialist past is imminent.

MUSSOLINI FROM 1883 TO 1914

He was born in Dovia, an area of the town of Predappio in the suburbs of Forlì in 1883, son of Alessandro (a smith with anarchist leanings) and Rosa Maltoni (an elementary-school teacher and devout Catholic). The maternal influence is evident in the decision to baptize the son, the paternal one in giving him the names Benito Amilcare Andrea, after the revolutionaries Juarez, Cipriani, and Costa. As a youth he demonstrated a violent and withdrawn character, soured by a period of study in a religious school, which exacerbated his rebelliousness. He studied irregularly and was suspended from several schools before earning his diploma in 1901.

From 1902 to 1904 he emigrated to Switzerland, where he took various manual jobs and frequented socialist groups. Returning to Italy, he began a career as a journalist, though he was also known for his oratory skills, and as an improviser, agitator and theorist of "direct action." His education and cultural preparation were summary, but he had learned French and German. He headed a few socialist papers in the Austrian areas of the Trentino region, as well as Forlì's weekly *La Lotta di Classe* (Class War); he wrote a short anticlerical novel entitled *Claudia Particella*; he emerged as the exponent of the Maximalist wing of the Socialist Party; and from 1912 to 1914 he directed *Avanti!*.

He opposed the Libyan campaign in 1911–1912 and was one of the instigators of the expulsion of the reformists from the PSI. The summer of 1914 saw his personal conversion to interventionism and his shift to the opposite side with respect to his internationalist past. ∎

The candidate lists for the political elections of 1919 are posted in Milan. In the Lombard capital, the Fasci di Combattimento *were also represented, but they obtained only 4,000 votes, demonstrating the lack of success of Mussolini's political initiative.*

Rome. The term *fascio*, to which Mussolini referred in 1919, was actually a recent term from Italian politics; it went back to the last years of the nineteenth century, which had seen the creation of various democratic or workers' *fasci*, as well as the Sicilian *fasci*: all of them movements or groups of a progressive and socialist orientation. The ideological connotation of the term shifted especially in the years of the First World War, to include the nationalist orientation of the interventionist *fasci* of 1914, the parliamentary *fasci* that called together disparate forces to sustain the intervention, the national defense *fasci* constituted after the defeat at Caporetto in 1917, and the Futurist political *fasci* of 1918.

The vague socialist nature of the term, subsequently tinged with a nationalist connotation, nevertheless represents approximately the ideological curve traced by Mussolini and his first collaborators, in a transition — from socialism to imperialism, from radical democracy to reactionary nationalism — that finds comparable elements in European politics and culture from the end of the nineteenth century to the First World War.

Mussolini had in fact begun as a socialist agitator and exponent of the Maximalist movement that obtained a majority in the Socialist Party (PSI) in the years before the war. In the autumn of 1914 Mussolini's position changed in the face of the European conflict in which Italy still retained its declared neutrality. The opportunism of Mussolini, and his movement toward ever more clearly anti-pacifist and interventionist positions, provoked his expulsion from the PSI. In 1914, with French funds and industrialist financing, the ex-Socialist founded the Milanese daily *Il Popolo d'Italia*, which distinguished itself with its fiery pro-war propaganda.

After the end of the war, Mussolini was still only a political soldier of fortune, an embittered journalist who hated the members of his former party and who tried to mobilize behind him the ample but still only potential store of resentment against democracy.

In March 1919, in a hall provided for the occasion by a group of Milanese industrialists and businessmen,

A group of fascists lays waste to the Milanese offices of Avanti! *in 1919. The* Fasci di Combattimento, *despite the vagueness of their political program, soon showed their true colors.*

AVVERTIMENTO?!

PADRON CHE QUI STAI
SE L'AVIDO FAI
PER TE SONO GUAI.
C'É L'OLIO LO SAI
E SU NEI GRANAI
IL COMODO E BELLO
GENTIL MANGANELLO

One of the first fascist posters threatens profiteers in the countryside with castor oil and a club. In reality, under cover of its revolutionary mask, fascist violence was directed from the beginning primarily against community centers, unions, and cooperatives.

with an audience of a few dozen, Mussolini launched the *Fasci di Combattimento* — "the combat squads."

With this description, the term "fascist" finally became clearer, to the point that its founder could say that the goals of the new movement were precisely defined by the name itself.

The official program of the movement, published only in June 1919, contained a series of platforms shared by other parties and groups, democratic, republican, and socialist. These included universal suffrage with the extension of the vote to women and proportional representation; abolition of the Senate appointed by the king; an eight-hour workday, and an extraordinary and progressive tax on capital. Beside these, there were glimpses of the significant catch phrases, such as the institution of a national militia in addition to the army, or the need for a foreign policy capable of "increasing the standing of the Italian nation in the world."

But in reality, no program defined fascism better than its effective acts. In January 1919, with groups of Futurist intellectuals and shock troops (the select and best-paid troops formerly employed in the conflict), Mussolini forcefully impeded an appearance by

Leonida Bisolati, former socialist and minister during the war, accusing him of sustaining a foreign policy of renunciation. The following April, the fascists, with the usual shock troops (*squadristi*) and Futurists, attacked and devastated the Milanese seat of the socialist publication *Avanti!*.

It was violence — given a standing on a theoretical level by Mussolini — that characterized the first political actions of the fascists. But still at the end of 1919, the movement was unable to take hold. At the general elections, the party was able to produce only one list, in Milan, and obtained only 4,000 votes and no elected deputy; in all of Italy there were only 31 *fasci* with 870 members, and in some places the *fascio* comprised only its one founder and member.

Fascism Takes Over in the Countryside

Having risen to power, fascism always tried doggedly to ennoble its dark beginnings, inventing for itself a sort of political and cultural lineage through the construction of an ancient genealogical tree of precursors. But the actual origins of the movement can be found in the war years and the years immediately following.

Hooliganism, violence, vandalism, and the exaltation

A fascist squadron in a clash with the "reds" in 1920. Violence and hooliganism, two characteristic traits of fascism, were not however sufficient for Mussolini to force his movement onto the Italian political scene.

of the values and "regenerative" myths of war were not sufficient to allow Mussolini to open a political space for himself during the so-called "Red Years" of 1919–1920. Only at the end of 1920 did fascism become a popular political movement. This temporal coincidence is decisive: the ebbing of the tide of post-war revolution and the increasingly evident signs of economic and political stabilization were preconditions for the expansion of fascism. This phase saw the first geographic and social transformation of the movement.

Significant fascist groups had existed only in the cities of Milan and Trieste, and in general the fascist sections had been created only in urban areas. Here there were political discussions and activities, and the outlining of platforms; the members could keep their affiliation to other parties, were often affiliated with the Masons, retained a common ground of past experiences — generally among democratic or socialist

IL POPOLO D'ITALIA

The principal vehicle of Mussolini's shift from socialism to fascism was his ownership and direction of the daily paper founded by him in 1914, only a few weeks after he left the editorship of the socialist paper *Avanti!*.

This brief lapse of time fuels numerous suspicions of corruption, but this doesn't mean Mussolini changed his beliefs due to pecuniary interests. He was financed by French interests with the aim of weakening the pacifist and neutralist front, and by certain large Italian industrialist groups interested in the increase of wartime production. The newspaper bears in its name the stamp of nationalist populism, mitigated by the original subtitle of *Socialist Daily*, changed later to the more vague but revealing *Fighters' and Producers' Daily* (*Quotidi-*

ano dei combattenti e dei produttori). Mussolini enjoyed a steady return from the paper, despite its very modest circulation. *Il Popolo d'Italia* was the trampoline that launched Mussolini toward a position of national notoriety, as well as an indispensable vehicle for his propaganda, in an era when newspapers were still the only form of mass communication. Before October 1922, the paper was one of the voices of fascist mobilization, along with other newspapers directed and owned by fascist leaders such as Balbo and Farinacci. From 1922 to 1943, the daily was the official mouthpiece of the regime and remained the private property of its founder, with the co-editorship of his brother Arnaldo and, after Arnaldo's death in 1931, of his nephew Vito. ■

groups — and did not in general differentiate themselves sociologically from the vast mixed ranks of the mid-level, petit-bourgeois citizenry.

At the end of 1920, furthermore, the fascists had been welcomed into the nationalist bloc, made up of various liberal elements countering the rise of the socialist and Catholic parties in the administrative elections.

The violent battle against socialist administration in the provinces and towns was the special terrain of fascism. It thus shifted from the major urban centers to the local level, and moved its armed *squadristi* wherever it saw an adversary to strike.

The leadership of the movement generally remained in the city, perhaps in a headquarters, from which it spread to the towns and rural areas. But for the first time, in many Italian areas (such as Alessandria, Pavia, and Arezzo) local agricultural associations created their own armed fascist squadrons. Terrorist actions thus extended into the entire area of the Po valley, to Emilia-Romagna, and into Tuscany. Above all, fascism made its appearance in southern Italy, in the particularly fierce form of the Pugliese *squadrist*i. Mussolini's political leadership was contested or ignored by these virulent and chaotic rural squadrons. In such areas there was no time wasted on discussion or elaboration of political goals; rather they were dominated purely by the impulse to antisocialist violence and the planning of the destruction of peasant leagues or "red" syndicates.

Mussolini at a rally in 1920. His political leadership was in this period often questioned by the local ras such as Italo Balbo and Roberto Farinacci, who moved their men autonomously and without awaiting orders from Mussolini.

The leftist nature of the first urban fascists was superseded by this political and social transformation. The protagonist of the new phase of the movement was the local militia leader, called the "*ras*" from the former title of the Abyssinian nobility. Fascist chiefs

November 1921: a poster announcing the third national congress of the fascist movement. It was on this occasion that Mussolini transformed the movement into the National Fascist Party (Partito Nazionale Fascista), in order to guarantee the better organization of his forces and the stronger political role of fascism.

such as Roberto Farinacci in Cremona, Italo Balbo in Ferrara, and Renato Ricci in Carrara emerged in this period.

1921: Fascists in Parliament

From the end of 1920 to the end of 1921, the number of fascists had grown more than tenfold, to more than 200,000. The armed movement claimed entire Italian territories, cities, and towns. These successes, unhoped-for even by the most optimistic of the *ras*, cannot be explained simply in terms of the superiority of the fascist military tactics over the unarmed forces of the socialist movement, or by the ebbing tide of industrial and agricultural unionism. The fascist attitude of the governing bodies and, in general, the complicity and non-neutrality of the State apparatus were decisive. The magistracy used a light hand with members of the *squadristi*; the army and the police armed them secretly; the prefects protected them and occasionally sent them on "punitive expeditions"; the liberals had already welcomed them into the electoral coalitions and the prime minister, Giovanni Giolitti, announced early elections in May 1921 in order to weaken the socialists, and officially included Mussolini's candidates in the nationalist bloc. It was in this way that the first thirty-six fascist deputies entered the Chamber.

III° CONGRESSO NAZIONALE
FASCISTA
ROMA   NOVEMBRE 1921

In the first half of 1921, an approximate tally counts 726 raids conducted by the fascists on community centers, printing presses and newspaper offices, workers' cooperatives, mutual aid societies and leagues, cultural centers, libraries, and even a community college (*universita popolare*). In that year, fascist violence killed between five and six hundred people; but one must keep in mind that for every murder there were approximately one hundred cases of violent assault: the fascists, who attacked in conditions of vastly superior numbers and arms, in fact tended to prefer to humiliate their victims rather than eliminate them physically.

The agrarian reaction that mobilized the managers and owners of large land holdings, the unemployed agricultural workers, sharecroppers, and small landholders united in their fear of the threat of socialist collectivization of the land, was however losing some of its momentum. Mussolini took the initiative again, transforming the movement into the National Fascist Party (*Partito Nazionale Fascista*, or PNF) in November 1921, and thus giving himself a more centralized focus from which to guide his organized forces, by now considerable, toward national objectives.

A census of party members at the time shows that among the fascists, 40 percent were agricultural laborers, industrial workers, and seamen, while the 60 percent majority was composed of students, agricultural and industrial professionals, businessmen and their employees. Comparing these data to those of the population at large, it is evident that fascism had obtained representation from the bourgeoisie and middle class

The fascists of the district of Verona gather in April 1921 for a rally in the capital. At the end of 1920 the fascists were admitted to the nationalist bloc beside liberal candidates in order to oppose the socialists and Catholics; but it soon became clear that they would not be satisfied with a secondary role.

in greater proportion than their national percentages. 90 percent of the fascist leaders were of bourgeois origin, and in May 1922, when the party reached 322,000 members, it was not only the strongest political party at the time, but in fact the largest popular party ever in the history of unified Italy.

After 1922, Mussolini commanded an organized force that gave him total advantage over other political competitors, and a good position for resolving the postwar crisis.

The Support of the Liberals

From all parts of Italy, fascists arrived at the Naples train station for a rally on October 24, 1922. In face of the uncertainty of the liberal political class, Mussolini was by now ready to claim the helm of government.

The instability of the government in the years 1919–1922 was evident to all contemporary observers. In the replacement of Vittorio Emanuele Orlando by Francesco Saverio Nitti, and of Giolitti by Ivanoe Bonomi, the time-honored political liberal class demonstrated its worn-out methods of government. There were difficulties with its generational and cultural

renewal, its wounds from the rifts between neutralists and interventionists, and the usual regional and personal rivalries.

Mussolini, on the other hand, had pinpointed the defects of the liberals and continued to deploy the double tactic of antisocialist violence paired with lawful reassurances to the upholders of the status quo.

He began nevertheless to vindicate the entry of the fascists into government, threatening with force those who opposed this design. But while he attacked the government as weak and insufficient against the antifascists (the "antinational" forces of internal subversion, as he called them), Mussolini ably reassured the king by renouncing, in the summer of 1922, the so-called "republican tendency" of fascism.

From February 1922, the Prime Minister was Luigi Facta, a person considered by all to be clearly a transitional head of the government. The vacuum of power that had been created could be resolved only by a government clearly shifted to the right, or by an antifascist coalition. To avert this second alternative, powerful forces set into action to clear a path for the fascists. Among these supporters were the owners and directors of major newspapers, high-ranking members of the army and navy, Masonic leaders, directors of the *Confindustria* (the General Confederation of Italian Industry), loyalists to the royalist party, and even members of the royal House of Savoy. All these forces pressed on King Victor Emmanuel III for a quick solution, in contrast to the uncertain and dilatory tactics of liberals like Giolitti and Facta.

Fascism was meanwhile in a position to mobilize ever greater armed forces, which the old exponents of the ruling class viewed with sympathy, perhaps deluding themselves that these forces would in turn be reabsorbed into the mainstream of the law and into conformity with the constitutional powers. In addition, the peripheral apparatus of the State in many parts of Italy was in the hands of, or closely tied to, the private army constituted by the *squadristi*. These were

A poster celebrating the years of punitive expeditions against the "reds." It is signed by Marcello Dudovich, one of the illustrators fascism used for its propaganda.

able to organize paramilitary parades and occupy entire cities, obtaining the removal of those few prefects who dared oppose them.

A belated attempt at antifascist mobilization took place in the summer of 1922, with the proclamation of a "lawful strike" by the *Alleanza del Lavoro* (the Alliance of Labor), constituted for the occasion by the General Confederation of Labor, the Union of Italian Syndicates, the Italian Labor Union, the Railway Syndicate, and the Federation of Port Workers. The strike, however, failed immediately following the attacks of the *squadristi*, and it was suspended on August 3rd.

On the 14th of that same month, the National Fascist Party demanded the dissolution of the legislature and new elections by November.

From Naples to Rome, the Road to Government

At this time Mussolini and other fascist leaders conceived the military maneuver that was later to be called the "March on Rome." At the same time they continued contacts and meetings with liberal representatives favorable to the entry of the fascists into government. In the

The doors of Rome, on the morning of October 28, 1922, are barricaded and guarded by the army. But Victor Emmanuel III had refused to sign the declaration of a state of siege presented by Prime Minister Facta, and the fascists were able to enter the city unopposed.

During the entire month of October 1922, armed rallies of fascists were held throughout Italy and addressed by the principal squad leaders. In Naples, during the great rally of October 24, Mussolini announced definitive action, without disclosing the tactical specifics. At the dawning of the appointed day, October 28, fascists in many cities took over post offices, posted guards at the railroad stations, and paraded before the army barracks and prefectures in a generally peaceful atmosphere and with the toleration of the military authorities.

The headquarters of the fascist action was in Perugia, at the Hotel Brufani, where the "quadrumvirate" was gathered: Italo Balbo from Ferrara, Michele Bianchi of Calabria, Emilio De Bono from Milan, and Cesare Maria De Vecchi of Piedmont. Mussolini, however, was in his Milanese office following the course of the operations, presiding over the political dealings of his emissaries in Rome with various representatives of the old liberal and monarchist establishment, and attempting to influence the decision of the king regarding the appointment of a government.

A first column of 4,000 fascists moved from Civitavecchia under orders from the Tuscan, Dino Perrone Compagni; a second of 2,000, from Monterotondo, was led by the Tuscan Ulisse Igliori; a third, of 8,000 fascists assembled at Tivoli, was led by the Roman, Giuseppe Bottai. Neither the army nor the police intervened to face the fascists, who did most of the "march" by train. Meanwhile, the previous day the king had refused to sign the declaration of a state of siege presented by Facta. The manuever demonstrates the efficacy of the double fascist tactic of violence coupled with compromise with the old ruling class.

In the following years, October 28, anniversary of the rise to power of fascism, was celebrated as a national holiday, and those who participated were awarded the certificate of the March on Rome, with associated honors and gratuities. ■

first days of October 1922, a fascist militia was created, with the Facta government unable to react to this open violation of the law. On the 24th, in Naples, a huge gathering of fascists claimed leadership of the government, with Mussolini constantly voicing his public reassurances to the King while preparing his plan for insurrection.

Mussolini's actions could easily have been thwarted by the Italian armed forces, but the king refused, on October 28, to sign the declaration of a state of siege prepared by the Facta cabinet. Facta then resigned. Victor Emmanuel III behaved as did many Italian conservatives, afraid that the eventual defeat of Mussolini would reopen the way for a political resurgence of the democratic and socialist forces. For the king, the only question with the right-wing solution was in entrusting power to new men.

The march on Rome ended with complete success; here, a group of fascists parades through the streets of the city. Many of the participants of the march on Rome traveled a good part of the way by train, demonstrating the low risk of the enterprise.

The actual march on Rome of the fascist columns (some of whom arrived in the vicinity of the capital by train, attesting to the low risk of the enterprise) was not at all an actual military maneuver, but was rather a form of psychological warfare, which created an atmosphere and sense of the general collapse of the State.

Outside the capital, the fascists had mobilized with more concrete results, with the occupation of post offices, railway stations, newspaper offices, prefectures, and police stations. The army, the magistracy, the *Confindustria*, and the bureaucracy learned with relief that on October 29 the king had charged Mussolini with the creation of a new government. To receive the commission, the head of fascism presented himself at the Quirinale wearing a black shirt rather than his ceremonial uniform. He was the first prime minister in the history of the Kingdom of Italy without an advanced degree, and also, at 39, the youngest. Installed at the head of government on October 30, 1922, he watched with satisfaction the parade of tens of thousands of fascists entering the capital, with the crisis by then resolved.

Benito Mussolini
Fondatore e Duce del Fascismo, ora Presidente del Consiglio dei Ministri.

The decision of Victor Emmanuel III was certainly rife with consequences, but one must not forget that the constitutional structure of the State permitted its highest officials to resolve political crises outside of parliamentary avenues; perhaps, as in this case, entrusting the formation of the government to the head of a small group of about thirty deputies.

Furthermore, the political and social penetration of fascism into the bourgeoisie and State apparatus was already sufficient to guarantee a solid compromise between fascist upheaval and the elements of conservatism in the events of October 1922.

There was not, on that occasion, any social revolution as the fascists would later claim, nor any dramatic suicide of Italian liberalism in the face of an unstoppable fascist insurrection. The reality is that Mussolini's rise to power — an expression that is much more historically accurate than that of a seizure of power – occurred in conditions of low risk, of strange semi-legality, and of the lucky (but certainly not inexplicable) success of a movement born only three and half years earlier.

Mussolini in the new garb of Prime Minister on a celebratory postcard from 1922. When Victor Emmanuel III entrusted the head of fascism with the formation of a new government, Mussolini was 39 years old. He was the youngest Prime Minister in the history of Italy, and the first not to boast an advanced degree.

Chapter 2

MUSSOLINI
IN GOVERNMENT

IN OCTOBER OF 1922, WHEN MUSSOLINI WAS ASKED TO FORM A NEW GOVERNMENT, THERE WERE MANY WHO THOUGHT THAT FASCISM WOULD NOT REPRESENT A BREAK WITH ITALY'S LIBERAL TRADITION. IT TOOK ONLY A FEW YEARS TO SHOW THAT REALITY WAS ANOTHER STORY.

The events of 1922 began what contemporaries, even before historians, would call the fascist *Ventennio* (Twenty Years). But this should not make us forget that fascism, which rose to power through mostly legitimate political channels, did not immediately set up an open dictatorship or a totalitarian regime.

For a few years Mussolini guided a coalition government sustained in parliament by heterogeneous forces. However, the break with previous tradition was evident. Indeed, alongside the official government, fascism installed certain new institutions that completely changed the conditions of the law and in some measure constitutional sovereignty itself. Mussolini furthermore made it clear that his was the dominant personality, and he moved with characteristic swings between histrionics, arrogance, respectability, insolence, and conformity to standards of order and stability.

If the royally appointed Senate voted its confidence with an extraordinary majority, the Chamber also contained many forces and parties sustaining Mussolini: from nationalists to various liberal groups; from democrats and radicals to the Catholics of the Popular Party. In practice, parliamentary opposition was restricted to the socialist, communist, and republican deputies.

Victor Emmanuel III and Mussolini during an official visit to Milan in 1923. Between 1922 and 1924, at the helm of a government made up of heterogeneous forces, Mussolini consolidated his relationship with the crown. Meanwhile, beside the traditional institutions of liberal Italy, he put in place certain innovations that were a prelude to the regime of the following years.

The government formed by Mussolini after the march on Rome of October 1922. Included were, among others, the philosopher Giovanni Gentile (public education), the military officers Armando Diaz and Paolo Thaon (war and navy, respectively), and the liberal entrepreneur Teofilo Rossi do Montelera (industry).

The Double Fascist State

In distributing government posts, Mussolini demonstrated his political prowess, reserving for himself the foreign ministry and the ministry of the interior, and filling a good number of the under-secretariats and directorships with fascists, in order to control the administrative machine closely and effectively.

But many ministries were also given to liberal, Catholic, and democratic party members. Teofilo Rossi di Montelera, a rightist liberal and businessman, was named as minister of industry, the philosopher Giovanni Gentile was entrusted with public education, and the military ministries were given to Marshall Armando Diaz and Admiral Paolo Thaon di Revel. Thus Mussolini enlarged the political scope of his supporters and

connections without renouncing the leadership of a "strong" government that he personally controlled, and into which the diverse forces of Italian politics were being more and more ineluctably drawn.

In 1923, the National Fascist Party fused with the small Italian Nationalist Party, which numbered only about a dozen deputies but had established its own armed *squadristi* — the "blue shirts" — who were particularly active in southern Italy. The fusion of the two parties was extremely important for the political and ideological balance of fascism in power. Indeed, from the nationalists came several of Mussolini's most important collaborators during the crucial transition from coalition government to dictatorship. Ministers such as Luigi Federzoni and Alfredo Rocco made decisive contributions to the construction of an authoritarian State, as well as to a conservative definition of the characteristics of fascist ideology.

But the relatively diverse organization of Mussolini's government in no way meant the restoration of civil rights to all citizens, especially not to antifascists. In December 1922, for example, the Turin fascists viciously murdered eleven people (some sources say twenty-two) and gravely injured twenty more.

At the beginning of 1923, the fascist *squadristi* that had dominated Italy for the two preceding years were reformed as the *Milizia volontaria per la sicurezza nazionale* (MVSN, the Volunteer Militia for National Security). Thus the private armed forces of fascism became legal, and the militia proved itself a forceful deterrent. On the one hand, it continued to threaten antifascist citizens, and keep surveillance on them. On the other, it made clear to Mussolini's supporters that he considered his government anything but transitory or defenseless. Under orders from the founder of fascism, the militia was commanded by General Emilio De Bono, who was at the same time the chief of the state police. This is an example of the double, parallel character of power typical of Italian fascism, and of other authoritarian regimes inspired by it.

The "double State" that began to form in 1923 had its open manifestation in the militia. Its secret one was in the *Gran Consiglio*: the Grand Council of Fascism. This clandestine institution, presided over by Mussolini, held secret nocturnal meetings that brought together groups of fascist leaders (the individuals differing depending on the circumstances). The purpose of the meetings was to control the deliberations of the official government, led by Mussolini but composed of ministers from other parties as well.

It has been said that the grand council acted as a "shadow government," but this definition seems inexact. A shadow government, according to the classic

Luigi Federzoni (1878–1967), leader of the Partito Nazionalista *(Nationalist Party), during a rally in 1924. The year before this small party merged with the National Fascist Party (*PNF*). A member of the Grand Council, Federzoni was to be among the signers of the Grandi Resolution which, on July 25,1945, marked the fall of* il Duce.

Royal Decree No.31 of January 14, 1923 instituted a "voluntary militia for national security" which was to be "at the service of God and the Italian fatherland, and under orders from the Head of Government.

"In conjunction with the armed forces for public security and the Royal army, and for the maintenance of internal public order; it prepares citizens and holds them in reserve for the defense of Italian interests in the world [...].

"Recruitment is voluntary and comes from among the ranks of the fascist militia between 17 and 50 years of age who apply for it and who, in the judgment of the President of the Council of ministers or of the hierarchical powers delegated by him, possess the requisite ability and morality [...].

"The militia for national security gives its services without compensation. When its services are required outside the city of residence of the detachment, it is maintained at the expense of the State [...].

"In the case of a general mobilization or of a partial call-up of the army or navy, the fascist militia will be absorbed by the army and navy in arms, according to the posts and ranks of the individual militia members [...].

"The expenses for the institution and functioning of the militia for national security will be included in the budget of the Ministry of the Interior."

The decree No.831 of March 8, 1923 specified that the Militia, "while maintaining itself strictly within the scope of its assigned duties, bases itself on the traditions of the fascist militia which increased the standing of victory and gave back to Italy its sense of glory and of national strength [...].

"Discipline consists of abdicating one's own will in order to submit to that of those delegated to command for a higher interest than that of the individual [...].

"The basis of discipline is the obedience owed by the subordinate to the superior. This obedience must be blind, immediate, respectful, and absolute."

And the Royal Decree No. 832 of March 8, 1923, demonstrating the political character of affiliation to the militia, added that "applications for admission must be presented to the director of the local *fascio* and passed by him to the provincial federation, which, always in accord with the Legion Commander responsible for the area, decides on admission." ■

form of British experience, is in fact an example of the democratic functioning of a parliamentary system with checks and balances. In such a system the acts of government constituted by the majority are submitted to the critical sieve and the counter-proposals of an "informal government," which, without actual powers, is made up of the opposition minority. Mussolini's official government, on the contrary, showed itself to be moving in the opposite direction, away from the tradition of parliamentary law. Yes, the grand council worked in the shadows, but in a new way, by which the fascists tended to occupy and guarantee for themselves every space of power, hidden and overt, thus creating a political situation which made any real opposition exceedingly difficult.

Mussolini presides over a meeting of the Grand Council. From 1923 on, this new body shadowed the official government, deciding the political lines to which the government and the parliament were expected to conform.
To the left, Mussolini marches with a group of Militia officials in 1928.

Mussolini's personality, and the conditions in which fascism began its control of the government, were together accelerating a process toward irreversibility, irremovability, and irreplaceability, and thus toward permanence in power, without restrictions or time limits. This gradual introduction of a tendency toward totalitarianism in politics was marked by unmistakable measures on the part of Mussolini's government.

Those social classes and power structures that had supported the entry of the fascists into government were immediately rewarded. The registration of stocks and bonds, which had facilitated fiscal accountability, was abolished. Certain services that had been nationalized with negative repercussions for private industry, such as the telephone system, were re-privatized. The state monopoly on life insurance was abolished, and inheritance taxes were reduced. Rents, which had been fixed during and after the war, were deregulated

Giacomo Acerbo (second from the left) prepares the list of government candidates for the upcoming elections in February 1924. With him are the other members of the commission appointed by the government, the so-called "pentarchy": Cesare Rossi, Aldo Finzi, Michele Bianchi, and Francesco Giunta (seated, from the left).

to benefit landlords who were thus able to profit from large rent increases.

The government furthermore began to lay off large numbers of railway workers, in part to lighten the public spending on an overlarge workforce left over from hiring during the war, but also in part to strike at the union base of socialism, and more generally at the democratic movement.

Education and Electoral Reforms

One notable measure of the early years of fascist rule was the reform of schools, promoted in 1923 by Minister Gentile and defined by Mussolini as "the most fascist of reforms." The changes swiftly undid

decades of democratic initiatives in order to affirm an authoritarian practice. These changes were made following the principles of an idealist philosophy, which turned on the central role of the "educating State." A required exam was introduced for all middle school students; the humanistic character of education was emphasized, to the detriment of the sciences; and in order to increase the standing of elitist educational principles, a number of technical and professional schools, which had hitherto educated students from the working classes, were limited or abolished.

Il Popolo d'Italia

Fondatore BENITO MUSSOLINI

giornale dell'Interven
to, della Rivoluzione,
dell'Impero, del Popolo.

The decree No.3288 of July 15, 1923 ordered that "the managing editor of a newspaper or other periodical publication [...] must be the director, or one of the principal editors of the newspaper or the publication, and must obtain the authorization of the Prefect of the province where the newspaper or publication is printed. Senators and deputies may not be managing editors. They cannot assume the position of managing editor, and those who have assumed the position will lose it if they are condemned more than twice for crimes committed in the press."

The prefect had the authority to give warning to the managing editor "if the newspaper or periodical hinders the Government in its foreign relations, or damages the national image within the country or outside it, or incites unjustified alarm in the population by means of false or tendentious information," or "instigates crimes, or incites class hatred or disobedience to the laws or the orders of the authorities, or compromises the discipline of public servants, or favors the interests of foreign States, organizations or individuals to the detriment of Italian interests, or vilifies the Fatherland, the King, the Royal Family, the Supreme Pontiff, the State Religion, the institution and powers of the State or friendly powers, by means of articles, editorials, notes, titles, illustrations, or cartoons. The Prefect has the authority to revoke the authorization of a managing editor who has been warned twice in one year...[and] the authority to deny the authorization of a new managing editor when the preceding one has been revoked or condemned twice in the space of two years to detention for no less than six months for any crimes committed in the press, or when newspapers or periodicals censured by prefectural provisions assume new titles in order to continue publication [...].

"Newspapers or periodicals published in contravention of the preceding dispositions will be seized. The seizure will be executed by the authorities of public security without need for special authorization [...].

"All crimes of the press or committed by means of the press will be prosecuted without delay." ■

On the occasion of the elections of 1924, a poster invites voters to cast their ballots for the listone, *the National List that comprised fascist candidates, as well as liberals (such as Vittorio Emanuele Orlando) and Catholics (such as Paolo Mattei-Gentili). Right, the socialist deputy Giacomo Matteotti (1885–1924) with other members of his party.*

Education became, in the following years, one of the privileged areas of fascism with its vast project of manufacturing consensus through cultural propaganda and ideological indoctrination.

But the most important reform, which, like many others introduced by fascism, can more rightly be termed a "counter-reform," was the electoral one that sought to guarantee Mussolini's fundamental objective of political "endurance." The law, which took its name from its first supporter, the fascist undersecretary Giacomo Acerbo, was approved by a large majority of deputies and passed, thanks to the abstention of the Popular Party, which had just suffered the affront of having its ministers pushed out of the government. The new electoral law guaranteed two-thirds of the parliamentary seats to the party list that received only a relative majority (at least a quarter) of the votes cast.

Mussolini's spite against parliament had already been loudly asserted on the occasion of the first presentation of his government, when he had insulted the Chamber by calling it a "deaf, gray hall" that could easily be transformed into a "bivouac" for fascist "detachments." Local administrations had furthermore laid the groundwork for introducing the new electoral system by pushing out presidents of provincial governments, and mayors who belonged to parties of the Left. The combined forces of the *squadristi* and the prefects, who had dissolved councils and committees and appointed royal and prefecture commissioners, eliminated these opposition figures.

Also in 1923, there were several local elections in which fascists so threatened the voters that the only lists presented were the fascist ones. When it came time for the vote, the militia guarded the polls, keeping antifascists from voting and allowing all sorts of violence and vote tampering. Having thus obtained a monopoly of the seats, in many places the fascists were the only "elected officials." And it was from among these that the prefects generally chose both the observers and the local chairmen for the national political elections.

Given this legal and political framework, the elections of April 1924 ended with a decisive victory for the fascist *Listone* (the National List), a single national ballot that included fascists, their supporters and allies (among whom there were right-wing liberal leaders like Antonio Salandra and Vittorio Emanuele Orlando, and Catholics like Stefano Cavazzoni and Paolo Mattei-Gentili).

On May 30, 1924, before an audience of fascists who insulted him, the socialist deputy Giacomo Matteotti made a bold speech to the Chamber in which he denounced, with detailed evidence, the violence that had marked the recent elections.

June 1924: the crowds gather in Rome on the quay of the Tiber where Giacomo Matteotti was kidnapped by a squad of fascists. The corpse of the socialist deputy was found on August 16 in a forest alongside the Via Flaminia, about thirteen miles from Rome.

The National List and the other minor fascist lists obtained 64.9 percent of the vote and with it 374 deputies (275 of whom were officially members of the National Fascist Party); all the other parties combined, antifascist or non-fascist, obtained only 161 seats, having been penalized not only by the electoral system, but also by the obstructionism, illegality, and violence deployed against them by the armed *squadristi*. The deep rifts that impeded a greater unity in confronting the electoral challenge further divided the antifascist parties among themselves.

If one analyzes the results, one can observe that the fascist victory had been particularly strong in Emilia-Romagna, Tuscany, and certain areas of the Po valley, and had been practically unanimous in the south (where the National List gained more than 80 percent of the votes). In the north, however, the fascists got only slightly more than half the votes, and in many big cities and industrial areas they remained in the minority.

1924: The Murder of Matteotti

In one of the first assemblies of the new Chamber, on May 30, 1924, with an audience of fascists who insulted and interrupted him constantly, the socialist deputy Giacomo Matteotti made a bold speech in

which he denounced, with detailed evidence, the violence that had marked the elections. His well-documented accusations, and above all his motion that the election results be invalidated, infuriated Mussolini, who was worried by reactions both around the country and in the newspapers to Matteotti's revelations. On June 10, a special fascist squad assaulted and kidnapped the socialist deputy.

The disappearance of Matteotti generated a wave of public dismay and indignation, even among those who had, perhaps disingenuously, supported fascism and particularly Mussolini himself, under the illusion that the leader was more moderate than his followers. On August 16, the corpse of Giacomo Matteotti was found hastily buried in a shallow ditch in a forest not far from Rome. It was certainly not the first political assassination conducted by the fascists, who in 1923 had killed the Ferrarese priest Giovanni Minzoni and assaulted the democratic leader Giovanni Amendola. It was, however, the first political kidnapping and murder that targeted a deputy from the opposition with Mussolini at the head of government.

Mussolini's political and moral responsibility for the crime seemed clear to many. The actual perpetrators were members of a select cadre protected by the police and connected to the entourage of the prime

A meeting of the Aventino, the group of deputies who abandoned parliament in protest against the kidnapping of Matteotti. Representatives from diverse political movements and parties participated in the secession of the Aventino, but their opposition was reduced to an impotent but heartfelt call to the king to restore the full legitimacy of the State.

minister himself. Mussolini did nothing to speed up the inquiries in the days after Matteotti's disappearance, and hindered by obvious difficulties, tried to minimize the weight of the evidence.

In protest, an authoritative group of deputies from various antifascist parties and movements abandoned the Chamber and set up a committee that took the name Aventino, in an allusion to the secession of the Roman plebs to the Aventine Hill.

The Aventino forces, headed by Giovanni Amendola, began a vigorous press campaign against fascism; but their political denunciation was weakened by being couched in an appeal to the king, whom they asked to recognize his error and reinstate the full rule of law. But Victor Emmanuel III, annoyed rather than flattered by these appeals, never wavered in his support of Mussolini, who within a few months was able to regain his political standing.

Toward the end of 1924, the *squadristi* reared their heads again, with demonstrations of violence that made some observers speak of a "second wave," which was considered and explicitly invoked as an example among the *ras*, particularly by Farinacci. The militia and the fascists who were intolerant of Mussolini's waiting game —or, in their view, his compromising — threatened a massive strike against the antifascists. Mussolini gambled that the opposition would be unable to sustain a lengthy ethical and legal campaign against the brute force of the fascist powers. On January 3, 1925, in a speech to the Chamber which historians consider the beginning of the dictatorship, Mussolini dared his adversaries to denounce him as the head of a criminal association, and assumed all the responsibility for what had happened (including the assassination of

Matteotti). No one dared to respond to these extraordinary admissions.

In the course of 1924, Mussolini faced the only serious risk of losing power during the more than twenty years in which he remained the head of government. The king's trust in Mussolini, which he reconfirmed, was historically decisive, and the murder of Matteotti went scandalously unpunished. Some prominent fascists implicated in the case, like De Bono and Giovanni Marinelli, were fully acquitted; others among the actual perpetrators of the crime were absolved some years later, while a few were condemned with light sentences that amounted almost to condoning their actions, thanks in large part to their defense lawyer, Farinacci, the former secretary of the National Fascist Party.

Toward Dictatorship

The events of January 3, 1925 allowed Mussolini to consolidate his relationship with the king, the army, and industrialists: those very forces that, along with the party and the militia, had chosen him in

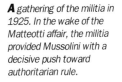

A gathering of the militia in 1925. In the wake of the Matteotti affair, the militia provided Mussolini with a decisive push toward authoritarian rule.

The senator Giovanni Agnelli, founder of FIAT, with the king during their visit to the new factory in Lignotto; beside the car, on foot, is the car-racing champion Pietro Bordino. With the events of January 1925 (which brought the electrical entrepreneur Giuseppe Volpi to the ministry of finance) Mussolini re-cemented his ties with both the court and the industrial sector, which had already supported him in 1922.

1922 and had not abandoned him in 1924.

The armed forces guaranteed their disciplined support of fascism, and were allowed to maintain their freedom from political interference in their internal affairs. The electrical entrepreneur Giuseppe Volpi, a capitalist magnate, became minister of finance and marked a shift from the preceding liberal economy, predisposing the incipient dictatorship to a protectionism that coincided with the interests of large industrialist groups. It was the beginning of an autocratic economic policy that the antifascists called the "privatization of profits" and the "socialization of losses."

Between 1924 and 1925, the liberals committed toward a national ideology moved en masse into the National Fascist Party. The government promoted the Vidoni Palace Pact, under which the *Confindustria* and the fascist unions exchanged exclusive recognition. The former Nationalist Alfredo Rocco became minister of justice and set his hand to the reform of the Italian judicial system. His 1930 penal code, whose provisions were authoritarian and extremely restricting of individual freedoms, remained in force in Italy (with amendments, of course, but without repeals) for half a century.

The true nature of the dictatorship was revealed in the course of the crucial two-year period 1925–1926: it was then that repression and reaction swept away any remaining vestiges of continuity between liberal and fascist Italy, and gave birth to an actual regime.

Unpunished violence and imposed order; discipline from above and the ability to instill among the masses an elementary system of aggressive and anti-egalitarian nationalism; humiliation of those who resisted or who appeared recalcitrant under the expansion of the police state; conformity of the powerful, who renounced their dignity to safeguard their profits; international recognition from conservative public opinion that magnified the figure of Mussolini and his merits: all these were shadows that began to form in the mid-1920s, only to grow ever longer in the dark night of fascist Italy.

Alongside Marshal Armando Diaz (1861–1928), who led the Italian armed forces after the defeat at Caporetto, Mussolini gives a "Roman" salute. Like the court, the armed forces supported fascism in 1925, giving their disciplined support in exchange for the government's abandonment of its plans for restructuring the military.

Chapter 3

THE FASCIST REGIME

IN THE SECOND HALF OF THE 1920S, FASCISM COMPLETED ITS TRANSFORMATION INTO A REGIME, TO THE POINT OF BUILDING A VERITABLE STATE WITHIN A STATE. FINALLY, IN 1929, THE ACCORD REACHED WITH THE CHURCH DEFINITIVELY VALIDATED THE ROLE OF MUSSOLINI IN ITALIAN SOCIETY.

Fascism repeatedly demonstrated that its transformation into an actual regime did not entail a renunciation of the political violence that was characteristic of its earlier activities. But the fascist government was able to pull off a sophisticated camouflaging act: just as it was setting up an open dictatorship, it appeased the social and economic establishment with its rhetoric of "normalization."

Mussolini presented himself to the eyes of the ruling classes as the only fascist capable of imposing discipline on the more intransigent *squadristi,* and as the indispensable mediator between the ruling class and the governing bodies. His public persona in these years was still far from that of the charismatic craftsman of the 1930s, years when he would fully embody the all-powerful authority of *il Duce* (the Leader). In the course of the 1920s, in fact, Mussolini was the target of several assassination attempts. These only succeeded in giving the government a ready excuse for introducing measures for the transformation to a complete authoritarian state.

The assassination plot of November 1925, which was uncovered in mysterious circumstances before it could be attempted, was ascribed to the former socialist deputy Tito Zaniboni; but the entire affair was probably a political maneuver orchestrated by

The facade of a Roman building transformed into an enormous billboard for the elections of 1934. As in 1929, the voters could cast ballots only with a Yes (Si) or No vote for fascism, which had by that time completed its transformation into an authoritarian regime.

Tito Zaniboni, the former Socialist deputy who in 1925 allegedly organized an assassination attempt against Mussolini. The plot was discovered well in advance by the police, and the real facts of the episode remain in question to this day.

the pro-fascist police. On April 7, 1926, an elderly Englishwoman, Violet Gibson, fired one revolver shot at Mussolini, wounding him slightly on the nose. Then, on September 11, the anarchist Gino Lucetti threw a hand grenade at the car in which Mussolini was being driven, but missed. Finally, on October 31, in Bologna, a pistol shot was fired at Mussolini, also missing its mark. Nevertheless, the alleged gunman, a youth named Anteo Zamboni, was savagely lynched by the fascists.

The Authoritarian Police State

It was in this context, between the end of 1925 and the end of 1926, that the one-party authoritarian police state, the fascist state, was born. The powers of the president of the Council of Ministers, now tellingly called the "head of the government," were greatly broadened with respect to the king and the other members of the government. The executive power was now able to establish laws directly, and this constituted a serious threat to parliament, and to the separation of executive and legislative branches. Furthermore, a new text of the laws of public security was passed, conferring unheard-of powers on the police forces.

Paired with these elements of authoritarian centralization was the final repeal of the election of local administrations. In place of a mayor, the *podesta* was installed, appointed by the king on the recommendation of the government. A law against secret societies was also introduced, targeting the Masons and sending a message to the Catholic Church that the regime was moving in a strongly anti-secular direction, while at the same time threatening any efforts of the antifascist forces to organize groups of clandestine resistance.

In Florence in 1925, one of the first antifascist broadsides appeared: *Non Mollare!* (Don't let go!). It was printed secretly under the guidance of Gaetano Salvemini and Carlo Rosselli, and was one of the many confrontations with the systematic and noisy limitations on freedom of the press that fascism was approving. The government made free use of censorship, and the prefects did the same with the seizure of newspapers. Pressure was directed both at the owners of the major papers and at Italy's most prestigious editors and journalists. The so-called "independent" press was gradually brought into line with the regime, while the dailies were quite simply suppressed.

Mussolini boards the battleship Cavour in April 1926, bound for Libya. The bandage on his nose covers the wound inflicted a few days earlier by a bullet from the pistol of the Englishwoman Violet Gibson.

The laws of November 1926, which were aptly called *fascistissime* (most fascist), declared the fall of the deputies who had orchestrated the Aventino secession. Many deputies, including Antonio Gramsci, were arrested; antifascist political groups and unions were dissolved and outlawed; a Special Tribunal for crimes against the State was instituted, with militia officials serving as judges; and the death penalty was reinstated and would be used against any antifascist condemned for "crimes of opinion." The abolition of the election of local officials and the return to the death penalty threatened to return Italy to the situation that preceded the liberal reforms of the late 1800s. The openly reactionary character of fascism was fully affirmed with the new police laws, which abolished basic human and civil rights, legal guarantees, and fundamental liberties.

Some commentators of the period, including the great French historian Lucien Fèbvre, who in 1921 founded the journal *Annales* with Marc Bloch, saw in the fascist laws a similarity to the repressive measures of the Sec-

Il Duce (the leader) derived his powers both from the acclaim of the fascist masses and from specific legal creations. The law of December 24, 1925 cast the almost absolute power of the head of government in Mussolini's image. He was no longer, as in the liberal period, a president of a council of ministers subject to the will of parliament, but rather the sole trustee of the king.

"He is nominated and his title revoked by the King, and he is responsible to the King for the general political direction of the government."

The leader was the ultimate organ of the executive power and chose his ministers, who were responsible both to him and to the king; he established the number of ministers and could himself assume the power of more than one of them.

"He is a member of the Council for the guardianship and care of the persons of the Royal Family, and has the role of the Crown notary."

Without his approval, the Chamber could not discuss any matter. He had the power to request that any proposed law, rejected by one of the two Chambers, be put again to a vote once at least three months had passed from the first vote, and he had furthermore the power to request that any proposed law rejected by one of the two Chambers be passed on to the other Chamber and examined and put to a vote by it. "Whoever intends an act directed against the life, the health, or the freedom of the Head of Government will be punished with imprisonment for no less than fifteen years, and if the intention is

acted upon, the punishment is life imprisonment. Whoever with words or acts offends the Head of Government will be punished by imprisonment or detention from six to thirty months."

The corollary to this was the law of January 31, 1926, which conceded to the executive power the ability to establish legal standards without any parliamentary control.

Mussolini explained the contents of the law to his ministers thus: "It is unnecessary to remind you that this law attempts to restrain the exaggerated extension of the powers of the Legislative branch — a pernicious tendency, current for many years and aggravated by various causes during and after the war."

"This law," he said, "defines completely the extension of powers of the Executive branch to pro-

mulgate judicial standards, by its own right [...].

"This law occupies a pre-eminent place in the program of legislative reforms [...], for it reestablishes normalcy and clarity in the relations between the Legislative Power and the Executive Power. It recalls the former to its proper function, and assigns to the latter the attributes confirming its particular character as the imminent and continuous power of the State — the guardian of its supreme, inalienable exigencies, the satisfaction of which is revealed to be of pressing urgency in the complex and multiform life of the Nation."

And in April 1937, Mussolini defined the law of January 1926 as "among the foundations of the Regime, by which, in every case, absolute respect for its laws is imposed." ■

ond Empire, and spoke therefore of "Bonapartism." Without doubt, the fascist regime did share some of the classic features of the old order, but it presented some innovations as well, as in the new military nature of the masses within the National Fascist Party.

In general, one can safely say that the most important element that distinguished fascism from previous reactionary and authoritarian regimes was its capacity to mobilize a modern mass movement and at the same time strengthen the traditional powers of the state. However it is important to remember the decisive importance of the transformations of the period 1925–1926, which were irreversible and indispensable to fascism's ability to stay in power. While the organization of the masses obtained its spectacular results later and as an element secondary to that of the sweeping "counter-reform," if one were to weigh them in the balance of history, the police state was always definitely of greater weight than the masses.

A session of the Special Tribunal for the Defense of the State, the court constituted in November 1926 and composed of militia officials. The task of the Special Tribunal was to judge opposition to the regime.

The cafeteria of the Perugina factory in the late 1920s. Between 1926 and 1927 the fascists prepared the legal and popular instruments necessary for a tighter control on the sphere of labor.
Right, the Secretary of the fascist Union, Edmondo Rossoni.

In the World of Work

It can be said that fascism suppressed the greater part of the foundations of a legal State such as that which had characterized the modern history of Italy and of Europe — but with the exception of private property. Mussolini's government introduced no elements of social or economic revolution; in fact, it made capitalism and fascism fully compatible and reciprocally functional. This assertion can easily be confirmed if one dips just slightly below the surface of fascist popular leadership.

The government abolished the ministry of labor as well as the celebration of May 1, for which it substituted the *Natale di Roma* (birthday of Rome) on April 21.

The judicial cornerstone of the new labor relations was the law of April 3, 1926, prepared by Alfredo Rocco, by which a special Labor Court was established to reconcile union disputes, and which, more importantly, abolished both the right to strike for laborers, and the right to lock-outs for employers. In practice, however, managers were given every opportunity to elude or ignore this rule. But, besides limiting every right to union association, fascism now denied the principal right of workers to strike and

punished any infraction on the part of factory workers or agricultural laborers with inflexible and persistent thoroughness. Furthermore, the single fascist Union, directed by Edmondo Rossi, could legally represent the totality of workers, including those who were not actually members of the union. All workers automatically had a mandatory union contribution deducted from their salaries. Thus a further financial blow topped the legal affront to the working classes.

The high-sounding declarations of the 1927 *Carta del Lavoro* (Charter for Labor) had no other goal than to mask the harsh reality of the facts with euphemistic and vague promises.

In the factories an iron discipline was introduced. After the political and union defeats, maintaining one's position became a primary focus in industrial centers, yet in fascist Italy the unemployment rate remained quite high, both in the cities and in the countryside, with emigration to the United States now blocked by various American policies. The real wages of factory workers underwent

THE PERSECUTION OF ANTIFASCISM

The physical removal and persecution of its political adversaries were among the axioms of fascist violence. This provoked among other things the phenomenon of antifascist refugees to other countries.

On this theme Law No.108 of January 31, 1926 prescribed in its only article that "citizenship will be lost to any citizen outside the country who commits or assists in committing an act directed to disturbing the public order in the kingdom, or from whom derives damage to Italian interests or to the good name and prestige of Italy, even if the act does not constitute a crime. The loss of citizenship is pronounced with a royal decree, on recommendation by the Minister of the Interior, in concert with the Minister of Foreign Affairs, after hearing the opinion of a commission composed of a State counselor, presiding, the director general of Public Security, a general director of the Foreign Ministry designated by the Minister of Foreign Affairs, and two appellate judges, designated by the Minister of Justice. To the loss of citizenship may be added, in accord with the opinion of the abovementioned commission, the seizure and in more serious cases the confiscation of assets. The decree that pronounces the seizure will specify its duration and the destination of the revenue from the assets. Foreign citizenship acquired later by the owner of the assets will have no effect on the efficacy of the provision for seizure or confiscation. The loss of citizenship incurs the loss of all titles, posts, and ranks belonging to the ex-citizen." ■

Below are several of the fundamental passages from the 1927 *Carta del Lavoro (Charter for Labor)*:

I. "The Italian Nation is an organism having ends, life, and means of action superior to those of the individuals, singly or in groups, of which it is composed. It is a moral, political, and economic unity, realized wholly in the Fascist State.

II. "Work, in all its intellectual, technical, and manual forms, is a social obligation. To this end, and only to this end, it is safeguarded by the State. The totality of production is unitary from the national point of view; its objectives are unitary and comprise the well-being of the producers and the development of national strength.

III. "There is freedom of professional or union organization. But only the union legally recognized by, and subject to, the control of the State has the right to legally represent the entire category of employers or employees by which it is constituted [...]; or to stipulate collective labor contracts binding on all those belonging to the category; or to impose on them dues, and to exercise on their behalf delegate functions of public interest.

IV. "In the collective labor contract is found the concrete expression of the solidarity among the various makers of the product, by means of the conciliation of the opposing interests of the employers and the workers, and their subordination to the superior interests of production [...].

VI. "Legally recognized professional associations insure the legal equality between employers and workers, maintain the discipline of production and work, and promote its perfection. Corporations constitute the unitary organizations of production and integrally represent its interests [...]. Corporations are recognized legally as organs of the State [...].

VII. "The corporate State considers private initiative in the sphere of production as the most efficacious and useful instrument in the interest of the Nation [...].

IX. "The intervention of the State in economic production will occur only when private initiative is lacking or insufficient, or when the political interests of the State are at risk [...].

XIII. "The duty of employment [...] is under control of the corporate organs. Employers have the obligation to hire workers who are official members of the appropriate trades, and have the power to choose from the rolls of that membership, giving precedence to the members of the Party and the Fascist Unions according to their seniority of membership." ■

an across-the-board decline rendered all the more painful by the accompanying absence of other incentives or concrete assistance programs. At the same time, however, corporate profits saw significant increases, and this, more than any other assertion, defines the nature of fascist "productivism."

The currency stabilization program pursued by the government fixed the lira's exchange rate at exaggeratedly high levels. The excessive strength of the currency was such that the interests of exporting industrialists were threatened; but by this demagogic move Mussolini satisfied the broader interests of the millions of members of the middle class, who were employed at fixed wages with small savings, and was thus able to capture their support. Mussolini was furthermore able to gain not only general thanks but also the more concrete support of international finance. The Morgan empire, and American bankers such as Leffingwell, were generous with assistance and with loans to fascist Italy in this period of international economic stabilization.

PROTEGGETE ED ACQVISTATE
I PRODOTTI ITALIANI

A National Fascist Party postcard exhorts the consumption of "self-sufficiency" products. In reality, the policies of economic protectionism, together with the demagogy of the corporate State, brought about a general decline in the conditions of Italian workers.
To the left, Mussolini in 1927 with Giuseppe Bottai (on his left), then undersecretary of corporations.

The Countryside Offensive

If fascism's reaffirmation of the existing social hierarchies had extreme consequences in the factories and urban centers, its effects in the countryside were even more brutal. All the victories, even the minor ones, won with the collective contracts wrested from the landlords between 1919 and 1920 were obliterated. Few of the scant union and assistance programs of which urban workers could avail themselves were offered to rural laborers. Landlords re-imposed quasi-feudal obligations and burdens that led some prominent liberal economists such as Luigi Einaudi to speak of a restoration of serfdom in fascist Italy.

It was true, however, that the laws that sought to impede or maximally hinder the freedom of movement of rural laborers did not have much success. Internal migrations continued — though hidden and silenced by official statistics — with the movement being from the south to the north and from the countryside to the urban centers. Notwithstanding Mussolini's impassioned declarations of the necessity of "depopulating the cities" or increasing the standing of "strength in numbers," fascism was unable to halt the secular tendency toward a declining birth rate and the depopulation of the countryside. These archaic "ruralist" concepts derived in part from Mussolini's awareness of the necessity of weakening the modern, urban, industrial front, where the majority of workers had remained deaf to the fascist word.

It was on this agricultural and economic front that the government launched its first propaganda campaign, the "battle of the wheat." Framing the issue in paramilitary terms, the rhetoric exhorted Italy to meet the goal of self-sufficiency in wheat production. For

Mussolini during one of the many "battles of the wheat": in this case it is the first wheat harvested in Littoria (now Latina), the city founded in 1935, south of Rome, as part of the reclamation of the Pontine swamplands.

anyone who keeps in mind the social conditions and the forced dietary habits of the average Italian of that period, this mirage of guaranteeing to each his just portion of Italian bread appears quite indicative of the regime's popular, and not simply economic, intentions. In fact, self-sufficiency in wheat production was never fully realized by fascism, and the policy of favoring wheat cultivation exclusively damaged other more specialized and profitable agricultural production. Nevertheless the propaganda goal of exalting the national product and self-sufficiency was achieved and the mirage worked: there is no image of Mussolini more famous than the photograph that shows him, like a simple farmhand, participating in the threshing of the wheat.

A 1928 poster advertises the national contest for a "Wheat Victory." Despite all the efforts of fascism, however, the goal of self-sufficiency in wheat production was never reached, and the incentives for wheat production to the detriment of other crops proved damaging.

A State within the State

Historians agree on the fact that fascism represented a less profound break with the past than it proclaimed when declaring the "revolution of the black shirts" of October 28, 1922 an epochal shift. Above all, it has been noted that the phase of the fascist conquest of power was gradual rather than concentrated in time, and marked by compromises and accommodations among the various components of the fascist movement. The apt symbol of the fascist sheaf became at the end of the 1920s the official emblem of the State, and as such was printed on stamps and official documents.

In the second half of the 20s, the regime consolidated its more specifically fascist political outlines. In 1926, a new party statute introduced the criterion of nomination from above and from the center of national and local political leadership. The pnf was on its way at that point to having a million members. Beside the party, the unions, and the militia, several typical institutions were created that developed on a mass scale, especially in the 1930s, such as the *Opera Nazionale Balilla* (the National Balilla Project, or ONB), a paramilitary program geared toward children between 8 and 14 years old; the Youth *Fasci di Combattimento*; the Fascist University Groups (GUF); and the *Opera Nazionale Dopolavoro* (the National After-Work Project), which provided recreational and cultural activities for workers. These organizations all saw huge expansion during the 1930s.

Mussolini's tactic of a state within a state — conquest of all state machinery and control of the instruments of power by specifically fascist institutions — was now achieved.

A *group of children participating in the National Balilla Project. In the early 1930s, the organization of the Ballila was one of the most important structures to which fascism entrusted the building of consensus, along with the Youth* Fasci di Combattimento, *the Fascist University Groups, and the National After-Work Project.*

With his characteristic tactics, in 1928 Mussolini sought to confirm the balance between fascist organs and those of the State by the so-called "constitutionalization" of the Grand Council. The word is misleading inasmuch as an actual constitution did not exist in the fascist State. Indeed the ancient Statute, conceded by Charles Albert to the Kingdom of Sardinia in 1848, was still in effect. Nevertheless, from 1928, the Grand Council of Fascism was no longer a semi-clandestine organization, but fully legalized, to the point that it became a pillar of the legal edifice of the State. It held refined powers and a political jurisdiction that seemed almost to infringe upon some royal prerogatives, such as the authority to express an opinion on the succession to the throne, a privilege jealously guarded and exclusively preserved, until then, by the House of Savoy.

The Accord with the Church

After the consolidation of fascism's relations with the monarchy and the military, with agriculture and industry (accords all forged by the heads of the ruling oligarchy), there was only one thing the regime needed to guarantee an authentic and lasting popular support: an agreement with the Church. The last step in the process of fascism's conquest and consol-

idation of power was indeed the signing of the Lateran Pacts.

On February 11, 1929, the deep rift that had opened with the Italian military conquest of the Pontifical State in 1870 was mended after the long and detailed diplomatic negotiations that produced the accords signed by Mussolini and Cardinal Pietro Gasparri. Thus the "Roman question" was put to rest.

The Lateran Pacts included a treaty that sanctioned reciprocal diplomatic recognition between Italy and the Holy See (a sovereign state with a miniscule territory), and a Financial Convention by which the Italian State compensated the Church for the material damages incurred more than half a century before. Furthermore, a Concordat was signed, and

On February 11, 1929, Cardinal Gasparri and Mussolini sign the Lateran Pacts. The accords of 1929 included a treaty that established reciprocal recognition between the Holy See and the Kingdom of Italy, a Financial Convention for the restitution of damages sustained by the Pontifical State in 1870, and a Concordat to regulate the relations between the Italian State and the Church.

After the signing of the Concordat in 1929 the new triad as depicted in public iconography shows the king beside the Pope and Mussolini, who, in the words of Pope Pius XI, had become "the man whom Providence has made us meet."

this clearly infringed on the secularism of the Italian legal structure and equally set itself against the ideas of *Risorgimento*, distant as they may have become. The Concordat extended the validity of Catholic religious marriage to the civil plane; it excused priests from military service; it extended mandatory teaching of the Catholic religion — defined as "the foundation and crown of public education" — to all the schools of the nation; it proclaimed the "sacred character of the eternal city" and granted a special status to the Italian capital, which was also the seat of the papacy, as an "international" capital.

The new triad depicted in public iconography showed the king beside the Pope and Mussolini; the latter, in the words of Pope Pius XI, had become "the man whom Providence has made us meet."

The advantages of the historic accord were reciprocal, but they developed in different ways over time. The Church, which had obtained a unique legal concession within the one-party State with the recognition of *Azione Cattolica*, the Catholic Action organization, set itself from that moment to the task of re-conquering civil society in Italy, a task it was able to continue well beyond the disappearance of fascism. (The Lateran Pacts were inserted, with Article 7, into the Constitution of the Italian Republic in 1948, and the Concordat was not revised until 1984.)

For his part, Mussolini was able to face with confidence the electoral test immediately following the signing of the Pacts. The farcical election of March 1929 in which one could only vote "Yes" or "No", gave more than 90 percent of the votes to fascism after a brief "electoral campaign" in which the clergy and particularly the parish priests of small towns had become active propagandists for the regime. Furthermore, the figure of Benito Mussolini became popular in the eyes of over 400 million Catholics around the world, and the Italian dictator was able to capitalize internationally on the image of an upright, reassuring, and pacific man, an image "guaranteed" by the Church's signing of the accords of 1929.

Pope Pius XI (to the left) blesses the crowds at San Giovanni in Laterano, the Roman cathedral, on May 25, 1933. It was the first time that a pontiff had left the Vatican since, in September 1870, Pius IX had chosen voluntarily to shut himself in the Vatican palace in protest against the occupation of Rome by the Kingdom of Italy.
Below, Mussolini and two priests give the "Roman" salute to the Pope.

Chapter 4

THE SEARCH
FOR A CONSENSUS

In order to enlarge the base for popular consensus, the fascist regime did not rely solely on violence and coercion. Mussolini refined his regime's propaganda machine: by radio, through mass demonstrations and sporting events, nothing was left to chance.

D uring the last historic years of fascism, the idea of the fascist "consensus" had become an impassioned topic of discussion both within and outside of Italy. A series of complex questions was examined that was reducible to the widely agreed upon notion that fascism, to retain power, should not rely solely upon violence and coercion. A debate that continues to this day was opened, which focused on the extent of commitment of many of the movement's adherents: their declared and undeclared motives, and their misgivings over a period exceeding twenty years. Decades later, highly polarized debates over this topic are still characterized by exaggerations, omissions, and distortions.

Furthermore, the term chosen to define the problem is probably not the most apt, from a logical or semantic point of view. "Consensus" is a term implying that fully mature political conditions — conditions characterized by autonomy and independence that foster the formulation of a political judgement — have been reached. While these conditions are guaranteed by democracies, they are certainly not characteristic of fascist regimes or dictatorships in general. In order for an effective and active consensus to arise, it is necessary that access be provided to information, and that choices from among sev-

*M*ussolini attends a gymnastic event at the Forum of Mussolini (now known as the Marble Stadium) in Rome. The emphasis fascism placed on physical education was one of the key elements in the movement's search for a broader support base; it was also an important stepping stone in the country's increasing militarization.

Giovanni Giuriati (center) with Achille Starace (right). In 1930, Giuriati assumed the position of national secretary of the Fascist Party, and initiated a wide-ranging review of the party membership in an effort to reorganize the PNF. His efforts failed, and in 1931, Starace assumed his post.

eral possibilities exist; these are conditions that the Italian regime has, historically, denied. Moreover, the fascists themselves, from Mussolini to the philosopher Giovanni Gentile, have always snubbed the term, maintaining that between force and consensus, force was the more politically indispensable of the pair. Instead of a consensus of a well-defined majority (which would, in turn, have implied the recognition of the existence, and therefore, the rights, of a dissident minority), the regime was interested in an indistinct unanimity, born of the acclamations of a well-disciplined and subservient crowd toward its omnipotent leader.

With time, fascism's powers of consolidation underwent a further refinement of the means by which, in the recent past, the faithful, and other members of the party and *squadristi* had been recruited. A specialized effort to engender greater support proceeded with hesitation: some steps forward and many steps back. Membership in the National Fascist Party itself was closed in 1926, but the attempt to transform the party into a more elite, better-equipped organization (from both the cultural and moral point of view) foundered.

Between 1930 and 1931, in fact, the national party secretary, Giovanni Giurati, conducted a thorough review of the party membership, expelling approximately 200,000 members. However, the hard feelings provoked by this policy forced Mussolini to nominate a new party secretary: the grotesque and caricature-like person of Achille Starace. In 1932 Starace reopened party enrollment, and in the years following, transformed the PNF into an enormous bureaucratic machine, in which members were forced to re-register often (for example, in order to participate in a public competition that would determine eligibility for a government career). The party's PNF logo, in the proverbial and disenchanted popular imagination, took on the meaning of *Per Necessità Familiare*, (to meet the needs of the family).

The Collaboration of the Intellectuals

In the area of culture, fascism distinguished itself by several concerted attempts to put together a consensus through the support of intellectuals. Mussolini had

Achille Starace (1889–1945) in 1931, taking field command of the Young Fascists in the Castelfusano pine forest near Rome. When he assumed leadership of the PNF in that year, Starace set aside Giuriati's plans for party renewal. He remained at the party's helm until 1939.

On the right: In 1933, Mussolini inaugurates the Congress of Fascist Cultural Institutes. Giovanni Gentile (1875–1944), who created and directed the Enciclopedia Italiana, *appears to his left.*
Below, a detail of the model of the EUR *in Rome, which was built for the World's Fair, planned for 1942. The Palace of Italian Civilization (top) and the Imperial Plaza are recognizable.*

already encouraged contact with the world of the artistic and literary avant-garde, especially the Futurists. He also set out to establish solid personal ties with nationalist intellectuals and those of the liberal right. By 1925, Gentile had written and published a manifesto of fascist intellectuals, to which Benedetto Croce prepared a reply, gathering, for his counter-manifesto, a collection of antifascist signatures that was far more authoritative. But there is no doubt that the force exerted by those in power, the growing authoritarian climate and the increasingly pervasive phenomenon of conformity, drove many intellectuals to collaborate with the regime.

The "old poet" Gabriele D'Annunzio, while kept at a distance by Mussolini, nevertheless, was hailed by fascism as one of its most illustrious forefathers. The most celebrated Italian playwright, Luigi Pirandello, declared his belief in fascism. The scientist Guglielmo Marconi served the regime and was repaid with positions of responsibility, including the presidency of the National Research Council (created in 1923) and the *Accademia d'Italia* (created in 1926). The greatest editorial undertaking was the *Enciclopedia Italiana*, whose aim was to gather all of the nation's intellectual forces within one

Because of an unexplain-
able failure to update,
the most widely recog-
nized national encyclopedia,
assembled with the support of
the regime and under the
dynamic direction of philosopher Giovanni Gentile, still has
a "fascism" entry signed by
Mussolini. Taken from the
volume of the *Enciclopedia
Italiana* in which it first
appeared in 1932, the text
was republished in numerous
editions and hundreds of
thousands of copies; in
addition, it was printed as the
preface to the new PNF statute
of 1938, thereby becoming the
basic foundation for the
teaching of the fascist doctrine
in every school. In this
"catechism" Mussolini exalts

violence, statism, and nationalism, while deriding humanitari-
anism, pacifism and democracy.

"The years preceding the March
on Rome were years in which
the need for action would not
tolerate investigations or
complete doctrinal elaborations
[...]. The fundamentals of the
doctrine were molded while the
battle raged on. It is also
precisely during those years
that fascist thought armed
itself, refined itself, and
proceeded toward an organization of its own [...]. The struggle
against liberal, democratic,
socialist, Masonic, and populist
doctrines was conducted at the
same time as the "punitive
expeditions." [...]. Fascism
today has clearly been singled

out not only as a regime, but
as a doctrine [...].

"As far as the future, and general development of humanity
are concerned, and aside
from any consideration of current policy, fascism puts no
credence in the possibility or
utility of perpetual peace. It
therefore rejects pacifism and
the renunciation of struggle,
which hide cowardice in the
face of sacrifice. War, alone,
leads to the maximum expression of all human energies,
and casts a seal of nobility on
the people who have the
courage and virtue to face it
[...]. Fascism, then, transports
this anti-pacifist spirit to the
level of the individual. The
proud motto of the *squadristi*,
"me ne frego" (I don't give a
damn), written on the bandage of a wound, is a philo-
sophical act that is not only
stoic: it summarizes a doctrine
that is not merely political; it is
the teaching of combat, the
acceptance of the risks that
come with it; it is the new Italian lifestyle [...].

"Love for one's neighbors
does not exclude the need to
educate them; still less does it
diminish the differences and
the distances that exist among
peoples. Fascism rejects universal embraces and, while it
dwells in a community of civil
peoples, it studies them vigi-
lantly and diffidently; following
them in their spiritual states,
and in the transformation of
their interests; it will not be
fooled by changing and false
appearances [...]. Fascism
reaffirms the inviolable, productive, and beneficial
inequality of man." ■

The new technology also worked in favor of the fascists. Mussolini, as early as 1924, was able to profit from Italy's introduction of radio.

unified work. In addition, the newspapers, as well as many cultural magazines — both new and old — were more and more inclined to exalt fascism.

By 1931, an oath of loyalty to the regime was required at all universities. Only eleven instructors in all of Italy refused to take this oath. Toward the end of the 1920s, the first faculties of political science emerged, in which the teaching and the appreciation of fascism and corporate ideology were promoted.

Several fascist leaders began to publish magazines. Giuseppe Bottai inaugurated the ambitious *Critica fascista* (Fascist critical review), and Mussolini, himself, was editorial director of *Il Popolo d'Italia*, and *Gerarchia* (Leadership, or hierarchy). University professors, professionals, and high-ranking members of the civil service (military, judicial, diplomatic and administrative) generally gave outward support to the fascist government, although many in these professions did not share the

regime's views and remained distant from it. Nevertheless, they were incapable of offering any real alternative, other than a lesson in dignified silence. Fascism's most enthusiastic supporters were students or unsophisticated young people from poor families. But in any case, while making significant and long-lasting contributions, most of the regime's supporters represented narrow social interests, closed circles, or intellectual elites. Thus, at the beginning of the 1930s, Mussolini's order of the day — "go to the people" — highlighted a necessity, but also constituted a confession by the regime of its failure to achieve a deeply rooted "popular consensus."

The Balilla and the organization "Young Italian Women" (Piccole Italiane), before the microphone of the Italian Agency for Radiophonic Broadcasts (EIAR). The EIAR became one of the primary propaganda vehicles for the regime.
Below, the cover of Radiorario, *the periodical and program guide of EIAR.*

Forms and Instruments of Mass Culture

If fascism could boast a high degree of organized support among the elite and upper, or ruling class, its penetration to the masses was much slower, more difficult, and at times contradictory. The inertia of the antiquated mechanisms of dependence and deference that characterized the lower classes; the paternalism and conformism reinforced by the government accords with the Church; the pall of indifference and apathy that the dictatorship seemed to cultivate; and the powerful, preventive control provided by the police all constituted bulwarks sufficient to dampen political and social protest. Among the more marginal, lower classes of the population — inhabitants of the rural periphery, and the illiterate — the regime was quite content merely to neutralize any subversive or basically rebellious instincts.

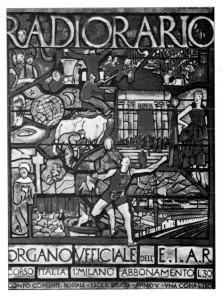

The new technology also worked in favor of the fascists. Mussolini, as early as 1924, was able to profit from Italy's introduction of radio. Perfected over the years, and centralized by a single state-run agency, the *Ente italiano audizioni radiofoniche* (EIAR), radio reached even the most distant villages. The voice of *il Duce*, the first Italian leader able to address the people, could strike with the fascination of a ubiquitous voice. He became accessible to the entire population, even those who could neither read nor write. The effect of the State's ubiquitous presence, made possible by means of radio, was probably more influential than any other instrument of propaganda. This explains why the sources of the time amply describe Mussolini's popularity, or cite the fact that, in some localities, peasant farmers believed the fascist leader to be the king of Italy.

One instrument that was quite successful in drawing the masses into the regime's orbit was the *Opera Nazionale Dopolavoro* (National After-work Project). Organizing for the first time the workers' after-hours

activities, fascism offered real advantages to OND members: discounts on movie and theater tickets, tours on "people's trains," a place where one could play bocce or cards. The *dopolavoro* was not a patently political organization, however; in fact the *dopolavoro* was the largest of the party's mass organizations precisely because of its apolitical character. The benefits of belonging to a labor union, or the party itself, were much more limited: gift packages were distributed to poorer children on the occasion of the fascist *befana*, "sun therapy camps" designed to improve the health of needy children who could not afford typical bourgeois vacations. Legal advice regarding retirement and sewing courses for young women in search of husbands were also available. In addition, subsidies were paid to families with a dozen or more children; such families were shown in portraits that today would be embarrassing, and regularly published during the fascist era to exalt the fruitfulness of the race. Meager as they were, the provisions the regime offered were appreciated by those who were able to profit from them within the domestic economy, an economy that was characterized by enforced frugality, if not misery, for millions of families.

*P*aris 1938: the Italian national team led by Vittorio Pozzo poses for a photo after winning the Rimet Cup. The regime's propaganda made use of the success of the national football team, which four years earlier had won the World Championship in Rome, and in 1936, had taken the gold medal at the Berlin Olympics.

In disseminating a mass culture made up of simple, strongly nationalist slogans, the fascist dictatorship's exploitation of sports cannot be overlooked. Soccer and cycling, with their national champions, nurtured the self-esteem and national identities of many Italians, who were proud of the victories of the national soccer team in the world championships of 1934 and 1938, as well as the cycling achievements of Learco Guerra and Gino Bartali.

Sports, and the fascist emphasis on physical education in general, were, however, also a means of imposing a growing militarization on civil society. The war-like rites enacted on "Fascist Saturdays," for example, occupied a sizable portion of time that many students would have preferred to have spent in less regimented diversions. Pre-military marches and camps that were administered by militia officers were greeted with little enthusiasm. Nevertheless, the regime obtained results from its

Learco Guerra (1902–1963) during his victorious Giro d'Italia in 1934. Fascism spotlighted the cycling victories of Guerra (five-time Italian champion and world champion in 1933), and Gino Bartali (winner of the Giro d'Italia in 1936 and 1937, and the Tour de France in 1938) to help generate fascist culture among the masses, as well as promote overseas propaganda.

Two examples of organizing consensus: a neighborhood festival in Rome in 1933, and a knitting lesson in a women's after-work recreational project during the late 1920s.

numerous parades and orchestrated demonstrations that were not wholly choreographed.

Finally, fascism understood how to manipulate folklore and fulfill the unvoiced expectations of many aspects of local culture, providing an outlet for genuine chauvinism at the municipal level. Beside the local traditional festivals, others that had been lost over the years were rediscovered, while still others were entirely invented. The occupation of every public space by the fascist authorities, in urban centers as well as the suburbs, was constant, and continued throughout the 1930s.

The new members who had been recruited with these methods of organized and diffuse propaganda, had in fact only a relatively superficial understanding of fascism. Nevertheless they were adequate for the needs of the regime, which based many of its hopes for unity on (1) its capacity to maintain a state of emotional tension, and (2) popular expectations that clouded the public's awareness of reality. Fascism cultivated individual immaturity and collective irresponsibility: not always able to deliver on its promises, it organized a permanent and highly charged circus spectacle instead. As long as the ruse lasted, and the game was able to maintain itself, the regime had little to worry about. In the meantime, it had at its disposal a monopoly on violence, and was able to repress those who continued to go without — those whose needs could not be met by the circus.

The "Third Way" and the Corporate State

Fascist ideology was based on a foundation that was essentially negative, in that it opposed existing values and principles, instead of formulating new, original and positive ideals. It has been said that this ideology —centered about nationalism and the exaltation of a tendency toward imperialistic exaggeration — had an eclectic nature, finding unity, as noted above, in its negativism. It was certainly anti-democratic, anti-socialist, anti-pacifist, anti-humanitarian, anti-liberal, and anti-parliamentary.

The ideological innovation that seems to have been fascism's most original contribution was the corporate state. With this philosophy, fascism attempted to give birth to a new way of organizing the economy and class relations, proposing a "third way" between liberal capitalism, with its market economy, and state socialism, as practiced in the Soviet Union.

Corporatism aroused interest and met with success overseas, especially in the years immediately following the global economic crisis precipitated by the Wall Street crash of October 1929. Moreover, fascism knew how to exploit the chameleon-like fascination with corporate ideology for its own propaganda ends. During the early years of the 1930s, fascist corporatism complemented the revival of traditional capitalism, which was grounded in a catholic form, and which had already been adopted in constitutional experiments both in Austria and Portugal.

The "fountain of wine" at Marino in the hills outside Rome during the grape festival of September 1928. The numerous traditions of local feasts and festivals (in some cases rediscovered; others, in fact, invented) were among the preferred means used by the National After-Work Project to create a broad base of support for the regime.

The royal decree of July 2, 1926 established the ministry of corporations; in this way a National Council of Corporations, subsequently reformed by the law of March 20, 1930, was brought into being. But it was not until the passage of the law of February 5, 1934, that the roles and functions of the corporations were defined:
They will be "presided over by a Minister or Undersecretary of State, or by the Secretary of the National Fascist Party, and will be nominated by decree of the Head of the Government."

With regard to the corporations, "a broad range of economic activities will be represented": the corporation establishes "the norms for collective regulation of economic relationships, as well as for the discipline of production within each unit. It has the option of establishing tariffs for loans and economic services, and setting prices for consumer products offered to the public under privileged conditions. It renders opinions on all questions of interest to the appropriate branches of economic activity each time they are requested by the Public Administration.
"The Head of Government may decree that, in certain cases, the Public Administration must request the opinion of competent corporations; the attempt to reconcile work-related disputes is performed by the Corporation through the offices of a College of Conciliation, composed of members of the corporation itself, who are selected from time to time by the president after having considered the nature and object of each controversy."
The 22 corporations were defined as follows: Grains; Vegetable, Flower and Fruit Cultivation; Wine and Oil Cultivation; Livestock and Fish; Wood; Textiles; Clothing; Metalworking; Machinery; Chemicals; Liquid Combustibles and Fossil Fuels; Paper and Publishing; Building Construction; Water, Gas and Electricity; Mining Industries; Glass and Ceramics; Internal Communications; Sea and Air; Entertainment; Hostelries; Professions and Arts; Social Care and Credit.
Finally, with the law of January 19, 1939, "the Chamber of Deputies dissolved itself, as the 29th legislative session came to an end. In its place, the Chamber of Fasci and Corporations was instituted, comprising components of the National Council of Corporations [...]. *Il Duce*, the head of the government is, by law, a member of the Chamber of Fasci and Corporations as are Members of the Fascist Grand Council [...]. The national councilors enjoy the prerogatives already established for government Deputies by the Laws of the Kingdom [...]. Council members forfeit their titles and responsibilities once the roles they play in the Councils, formed by members of the Chamber of Fasci and Corporations, also decline [...]. The work of the Senate of the Kingdom, and of the Chamber of Fasci and Corporations is split into distinct legislative sessions. The end of each session is established by Royal Decree, as proposed by *il Duce*, Head of the government [...]. "For the exercise of ordinary legislative function, the two Assemblies are periodically called into session by *il Duce*, the head of the government." ∎

We must ask ourselves, however, what the corporate system, as practiced in fascist Italy, really was.

As early as 1926, the fascist government had created a new ministry of corporations, without specifying its duties and prerogatives. The government's aim was to give birth to corporations that were only instituted later. In 1930, a National Council of Corporations was created, but it was not until 1934 that 22 corporations, which constituted together the so-called "representation of interests," saw the light. Finally, in 1939, the Chamber of Deputies became the Chamber of Fasci and Corporations.

With regard to the normal functioning of the Corporations, they actually produced very little in the way of jurisprudence, and generally speaking worked on matters that were limited and marginal in nature. The func-

An allegorical image of the Credit Corporation, in one of the wall-hangings designed by Ferruccio Ferrazzi in 1932 for the Palace of Corporations in Rome. Although planned in 1926, the work, which depicts the 22 corporations representing a broad spectrum of industrial production categories, was only completed in 1934. To the left, the main hall of the Palace of Corporations.

The functions of the corporate system were always essentially advisory; the corporate state eroded neither private ownership of the means of production nor the control that the powerful capitalist groups continued to exert over the economy.

tions of the system remained essentially advisory. Further, the corporate state did not erode, even minimally, private ownership of the means of production, or the control that large capitalist groups exercised over the economy. Even interventions by the state itself in the industrial and financial sectors, were brought about through initiatives on the part of agencies that were separate from corporate structures. Thus, ideological and propaganda influences held much greater sway than the purely economic and practical.

A mystifying aspect of corporatism lay in its pretense of being able to mask class conflict for the "superior benefit of the nation." The concept of *pariteticità* —referring to equality of representation — contained within it a number of curious elements. An early practical experi-

ment in the corporate system took place at the local level with the reinstitution of municipal or town councils, which worked beside mayors nominated by the monarchy after 1926. In place of elected communal councils, the prefects nominated councilors who were chosen based on the principle that the number of representatives of providers of work had to equal the number of workers' representatives. But among the latter, one-third of the places were reserved for professional people. Two representatives of the industrialists were to sit beside two industrial workers' representatives (who, themselves, were enrolled in fascist labor unions). Sounds equal, but in practice this meant that, for example, a few dozen industrialists would have the same number of representatives as the thousands of workers who resided in that particular community; a hundred land owners might have same number of council members as several thousand small farmers.

Above, Mussolini in 1932, with Giovanni Agnelli at the unveiling of the "Balilla," the first Italian economy car.
Galeazzo Ciano (on the left) is accompanied by Alberto Pirelli, who, during the 1920s and 30s, headed the industrial sector for rubber and its derivatives.

An Instrument of Propaganda

This form of parity of economic interests introduced a mechanism that was entirely contrary to contemporary electoral tendencies toward proportional, representative democracy based on universal suffrage.

Within the corporations themselves criteria analogous to those of the municipal councils were in force. Representatives of the owners in a determined area of produc-

The corporatist system did not produce concrete results relating to the economic or military aspects of war-related production, but did serve to mobilize many — in particular, students and young intellectuals, who were searching for identity and recognition as they were being psychologically prepared for a climate of permanent war.

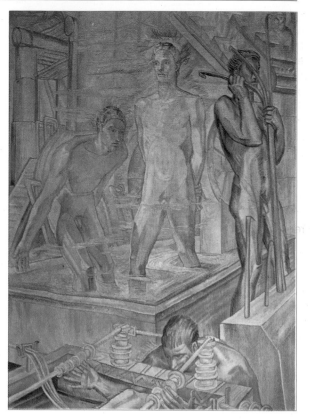

tion were entitled to a number of places equal to those held by the workers' representatives in that same sector. But this did not signify that the working classes enjoyed rights equal to those of the entrepreneurs, or that the interests of the workers had been elevated to the same rank as those of the owners; nor did it mean that the fascist state had actually achieved conciliation between the classes.

Within the corporations, in fact, representatives of the working classes were never manual laborers; they never truly belonged to the working world that they were charged with representing; rather, they were fascist unionists or professional politicians, nominated to their positions precisely because they would defer to the decisions that the more powerful forces, the representative of the owners, would dictate.

The excessive power of the private capitalist groups was such that they were able to delay or impede deliberation on matters they opposed. The practice that in the end came to prevail, was that the government and *Confindustria* would agree on certain concrete questions, often ignoring or omitting consultative input by the corporations.

Notwithstanding this negligible practical impact, corporatism had a great theoretical influence that went beyond its tranquilizing nature as a remedy against class struggle.

Corporatism served to legitimate the anxious attempts by many young fascists to give a positive meaning to the ideology of the regime. Acting as a means to reaffirm the international primacy of Italian civilization for posterity; recuperating the ancient glories of classical times and promoting the logic of harnessing all of the country's productive energies into an increasingly functional and self sufficient unit, it aimed at meeting the incipient needs of fascist imperialism. The influence of the corporate state did not produce concrete results relating to the economic or military aspects of war-related production, but it did serve to mobilize many - in particular, students and young intellectuals - who were searching for identity and recognition even as they were being psychologically prepared for a climate of permanent war.

Mussolini speaks to workers at FIAT. *Notwithstanding fascism's promises regarding the role of the corporate state, the arrangement that came to prevail during the '20s and '30s until the outbreak of war was direct collaboration between the regime and* Confindustria, *which omitted consultation with the corporations.*
At the left, "Corporation of Industry," one of the wall-hangings designed by Ferruccio Ferrazzi in 1932 for the Palace of Corporations.

Chapter 5

ITALY IN
BLACK SHIRTS

IN SPITE OF ALL ITS EFFORTS TO MONOPOLIZE EVERY AREA OF POWER, IN REALITY THE REGIME NEVER ACHIEVED ANYTHING MORE THAN AN IMPERFECT TOTALITARIANISM. THE COUNTRY RESPONDED AT TIMES WITH OPPOSITION, BUT MORE OFTEN WITH INDIFFERENCE.

Even during the initial phases of consolidation of power, the fascist regime displayed fully the contradiction between words and deeds, between propaganda and results. This would become one of the fundamental causes of its "crisis of consensus" during the early 1940s. If fascism needed to broaden its base of mass support to solidify and enhance its role among the various elements that composed the regime's historic bloc, it was not, in any case, able to appeal to the autonomous initiative of the masses, nor educate them to what may be called political maturity. The masses, then, were to be composed of dominated followers or "flocks," who were deprived of their individual personalities, and directed to make any sacrifice to advance the ends that the guiding light of fascism strove to achieve.

Such an orchestration of power naturally clashed with the reality of the needs and demands of the Italian population, elementary and basic as they were. But possibly even before its experience in this sphere, which certainly is fundamental, the fascist regime manifested clear limits in introducing its largely imperfect version of totalitarianism in the areas of public order and political life.

Mussolini during the distribution of "certificates of appreciation for service to the regime" at Littoria. During the 1930s, fascism intensified its efforts to attract broad support for the regime from the Italian populace.

Imperfect Totalitarianism

During the period between the world wars, every European fascist dictatorship was characterized by a tendency toward totalitarianism. This was intended as a monopolistic occupation of every area of power, as well as a single-party organization of every portion and sector of civil society. Based on the elements we have already, in part, delineated, it is clear that Italian Fascism had grafted itself and thrived on the rootstock of the monarchist and centralizing state.

The symbiosis between the old and the new, which functioned so well in the construction of the regime, was in itself an obstacle to the more complete conversion to fascism that a truly totalitarian framework would have brought about. Totalitarian design would have presumed an active party role, including its preeminence over the state; but in reality, events were traveling in precisely the opposite direction. From October 1922, it was the government, instead of the party, that was the generator of fascist policy. Moreover, totalitarianism would have implied a liquidation, however progressive, of the institu-

A group of Giovani italiane *(young Italian women) with Augusto Turati, secretary of the National Fascist Party from 1926 to 1930.*

tional form of the state — the diarchy that Mussolini would denounce only after the collapse of 1943. Unlike Hitler who, during the transition between the democratic republic of Weimar and the Third Reich, was able to accumulate the titles of party chief, head of the government and head of state, Mussolini remained institutionally beholden to the king, since it was the king who personified the position of sovereignty.

It was Victor Emmanuel III, rather than *Il Duce*, who received heads of state on official visits, and received the titular accolades of Emperor of Ethiopia and King of Albania after the fascist conquests of 1936 and 1939. The conferring in 1939 of the newly invented title of First Marshal of the Empire on both the king and Mussolini was one of the few occasions on which the two figures were placed on equal footing. The Royal March, the national anthem, preceded the musical execution of the fascist hymn, *Giovinezza*. The only new magistrates who were entirely taken from the ranks of the fascists were those proposed for the Special Tribunal. It was only with the "28ists" — men who at least had gained experience within the party and been promoted to state posts in 1928 — that fascism could partially renovate prefectural and diplomatic posts. It would be necessary to wait until 1936 and the arrival of Galeazzo Ciano at the foreign ministry to witness a more evident changeover in leadership, one that would satisfy the most ardent desires of fascism's advocates.

Mussolini's government worked for many years with the old bureaucratic structures of the state; this was especially true for the armed forces. Within the army and the navy, holding high rank was a way to gain favoritism, though shortcuts were made possible by privileged relationships with *Il Duce*. But generally speaking, cases of professional fascist politicians who entered the ranks of the military to the detriment of older (career) generals and admirals were indeed rare. More typical was the fascist presence in the new air force, to which the regime dedicated much attention, placing at its head the

Mussolini in the uniform of the "Imperial Marshal." This new title was conferred on both Il Duce and the king in 1938, and it was the only title that attributed to Mussolini a stature equal to that of King Victor Emmanuel III, who, in his role as sovereign, retained a formal primacy over Il Duce. Fascism, in fact, never succeeded in eliminating the institutional framework of the Italian monarchy.

The seaplane airport of Orbetello, in June 1933: Italo Balbo inspects the crews of the SIAE Marchetti hydroplanes several days before their second Atlantic crossing. Italo Balbo (1896–1940), who two years earlier had already flown the south Atlantic with twelve hydroplanes, was preparing a squadron of 24 planes to cross the north Atlantic in celebration of the tenth anniversary of the Italian Air Force (Aeronautica).

transatlantic flyer Italo Balbo, who was later named governor of Libya. But in the colonial area also, promotions of fascists took place in groups that included well-paid and well-trained career civil and military functionaries, who usually had received their training in the pre-fascist epoch.

The men of the "old Italy," furthermore, remained in control of the economy through the Bank of Italy, as well as the new agencies that had been created to reinforce and expand the public sector during the great depression: both the *Instituto mobiliare italiano* (Italian Securities Institute, or IMI), created in 1931, and the Institute for Industrial Reconstruction (IRI) in 1933, continue to function today. The banking reform act of 1936, like the 1938 law (which also continues to be in place in Italy), were the work of technicians and "high servants" of the state, whose staffs were well-versed in theories rooted in fascist corporatism.

Furthermore, neither the PNF (National Fascist Party), nor the other organs of the regime devoted particular attention to the training of personnel who would be capable of filling posts in the various sectors of state bureaucracy. The absence of a new director-class of technicians and politicians trained in modern economic practice, international relations, or administrative practice was lamented, even by fascist leaders such as Giuseppe Bottai.

Reciting the oath of the Young Fascist Women, at the opening of a rally in Rome (1934.)

A likely reason for this shortcoming lay in the enormous ego of Mussolini, who like Hitler, showed himself to be a megalomaniac centralizer of responsibilities, and extremely jealous of every other fascist leader capable of eclipsing his prestige for even a moment. In truth, the regime, through the unstated but evident will of *Il Duce*, failed to prepare for any serious change in the eventual composition of the political class, let alone pose itself the task of formulating criteria for an eventual successor to Mussolini. Thus, the regime contradicted, in principle, the trend toward totalitarianism by failing to provide itself with a long-range perspective.

A Silent Resistance

After the signing of the Lateran Pacts, fascism was obliged to contend with the active presence of the Church in Italian society.

In 1931, a violent argument erupted between fascist youth groups and Catholic Action (*Azione Cattolica*), an organization that while not being permitted to deal explicitly with politics, presented a challenge to the regime in the critical sector of youth education. The conflict was kept under control through the intervention of the fascist leadership and Vatican authorities, which imposed further limits on Catholic Action, restricting its activities to the area of religious education only. However, in many traditionally Catholic localities, young university students continued to prefer to enroll in the FUCI (Federation of Catholic Universities), rather than GUF (University Fascist Groups). Unlike the party, which seemed always to be submerged in its own bureaucracy and in spectacular projects, the Church expressed an exemplary capacity to form a directing class of its own, one that was active on both social and cultural fronts.

In the short term, to be sure, the regime maintained stricter control over the propaganda manipulation of youthful enthusiasm, but in the medium-to-long term, the Church's influence counted for more. Even in various cultural initiatives, as for example the *Enciclopedia Italiana*, ecclesiastic revision and censorship could act on fascist authors whose formative years had been influenced by Gentile or other liberal-conservatives of lay inspiration.

Naturally, the mass education of the population incorporated the regime's new policy in scholastic texts, which had passed through the double scrutiny of State and Church. But within this climate of agreement, an element of friction and rivalry persisted. The more solid force of [Catholic] tradition meant that many would turn willingly to the priest in moments of need, or to ask advice; moreover, parishes were becoming modernized, and their radios and film projectors compared favorably with those in the "after-work" circles and the PNF itself. Also children and young-to-middle-aged women attended Catholic Women's Groups in numbers roughly equivalent to those of corresponding fascist organizations. The Church, then, reinforced its influence among the masses without giving them an antifascist education. Some Catholic scholars described this phenomenon as "afascism," a term indicative of the incompleteness and imperfection of fascist totalitarianism.

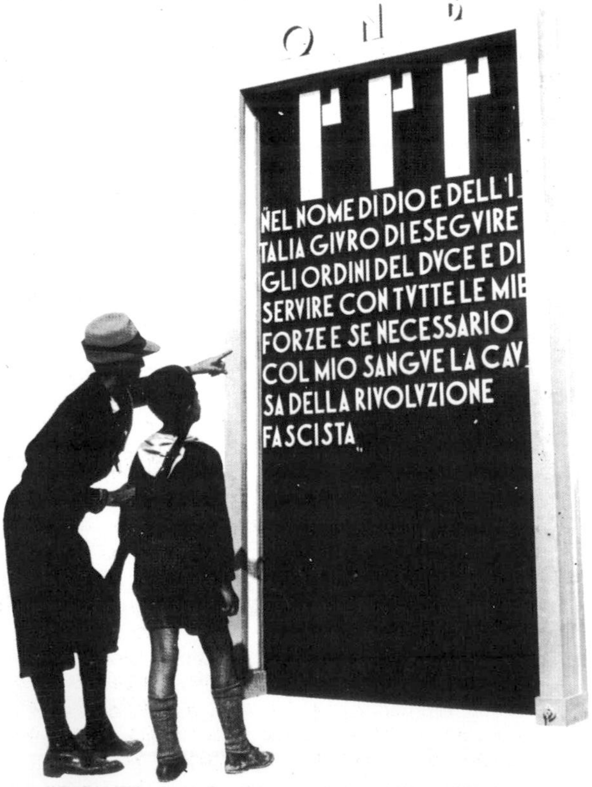

The capillary-like penetration of totalitarianism throughout Italian society was blocked by the societal characteristics of the fascist regime, which impeded a full and harmonic inter-class synthesis between the interests of the oligarchs and those of the popular and middle classes.

NEL NOME DI DIO E DELL'I
TALIA GIVRO DI ESEGVIRE
GLI ORDINI DEL DVCE E DI
SERVIRE CON TVTTE LE MIE
FORZE E SE NECESSARIO
COL MIO SANGVE LA CAV
SA DELLA RIVOLVZIONE
FASCISTA

The 1932 statute of the National Fascist Party signaled the beginning of the regime's policy of "going to the people," in an attempt to increase membership in its mass organizations. "The PNF is a civil militia, at the orders of *il Duce*, in the service of the fascist state [...]. The pnf is composed of fascist combat units that are grouped by province under the Federation of Fighting Fascists (*Federazione di Fasci di Combattimento*). The secretary of the FFC is authorized, as he deems necessary, to organize these groups into neighborhood units, or subsections [...]. In each provincial capital, a *Gruppo Universitario Fascista* (University Fascist Group) is established. With each *Fascio di Combattimento*, a *Fascio Giovanile* (Young Fascist) combat group and a *Fascio Femminile* (Fascist Women's Group) are established. The last in turn will form a group of *Giovani fasciste* (Young Fascist Women). Within the Federations of Fascist Combat groups provincial associations overseeing public education, public employment, railroad, post and telegraph, state-run industry, and the medical districts of the public employment agency are instituted [...]. The *Camicia Nera* (Black Shirt) constitutes the fascist uniform and must be worn only when prescribed [...]. The PNF, through hierarchical and collegial organs, functions under the guidance of *il Duce* and according to the directives provided by the Grand Council [...]. Responsibility for carrying out directives, commands or charges will be entrusted to

Black Shirts who have fought or worked for the Revolution, or to Fascists who have come up through the youth organizations [...]. On April 21, the anniversary of the birth of Rome, and the workers' holiday, the fascist draft will take place. The fascist draft consists of the marching of the *Balilla* through the ranks of the Vanguard and of the Vanguard through the ranks of the Young Fascists, as well as the passage of these last through the PNF and the MVSN."

Youths entering the PNF take the following oath: "In the name of God and Italy, I promise to execute the orders of *il Duce* and to serve with all my strength, and, if necessary, my blood, the cause of fascist revolution."

"The fascist who falls short of performing his duty," the statute continues, "through lack of discipline or deficiency in the qualities that constitute the [...]

fascist spirit, must be, except in cases of absolute urgency, referred by the federal secretary to the federal disciplinary commission. In extreme cases, the sanction is imposed by the federal secretary [...]. The fascist [...] who is expelled from the PNF will be barred from public life [...]. Those who bear public responsibilities in the name of the government may not be subject to disciplinary procedures or punishments until they have given up those charges [...]. Membership in the PNF becomes honorary in the following cases [...]: (a) of those who have been seriously wounded or disabled in war; (b) of those who have been wounded or disabled by their service to fascism; (c) of families of fallen fascists; (d) of party members who are fathers with seven or more children." ■

*M*ussolini with workers employed in the reclamation of the Pontine marsh. In 1932, with the construction of the city of Littoria and the reclamation of a large region south of the capital, fascism was trying to attract greater support among farmers and industrial workers.

The party and militia had even recruited elements among the urban and rural proletariat, but statistically speaking these were only a small group occupying the marginal fringes of the laboring classes, who comprised nearly two-thirds of the working population. Between 1921 and 1922, the fascists had grown precisely in those areas that, historically, had been grounded in workers' and farmers' movements with socialist leanings. But the violence, and the repressive and authoritarian discipline introduced by the regime, had naturally left a trail of wounds that did not heal, as well as regrettable after-effects. Many of the millions of workers and farmers who were averse to fascism expressed their dismay in the form of passive resistance or moral aversion, manifested perhaps only in silence.

The prevalence among large masses of the population toward an attitude that was politically backward — suspended between rare subversive demonstrations and inert apoliticism — resulted from the military successes of the *squadristi* and the policies of police-state dictatorship. But the regime failed to conquer the souls of many formerly militant socialists, communists, and anarchists, who continued to think for themselves, apparently impervious to the enticing allure of fascist propaganda.

Thus, the May Day celebration, which had been officially abolished, continued to be celebrated in private, with modest but convivial get-togethers among friends and acquaintances of like opinion. A few red flags would appear spontaneously, on the campanile of a church or the highest tree on a hill. Graffiti disrespectful of *Il Duce* would appear overnight on the facades of public buildings and fascist headquarters.

Meanwhile rumors against corrupt leaders, protest marches by women demonstrating for bread and work in front of the municipal buildings, mean-spirited jokes about the contradictory behavior and misdeeds of the regime, signaled the presence of an independent spirit among the populace. Rifts between former rivals began to close as the politically naive but psychologically acute perception grew that fascism represented a hostile and dangerous force. At the foundation of this "reactionary regime of the masses," were millions of individuals who were concerned, perplexed, and discontented: the totalitarian state, in theory, should have made efforts to win their unconditional faith, but contented itself, in practice, with their silence.

The Many Faces of Antifascism

To many outside observers, fascism conveyed the impression of a highly popular regime, one that seemed to arouse the enthusiasm of the masses with gigantic manifestations and "seas of faces," especially on occasions such as public festivals, special events, and rallies announced by *Il Duce*. In the prosaic and less ostentatious reality of everyday life, however, the regime

Mussolini, with Starace (left) and Ciano (right, in militia uniform), in July 1934, during a rally of religious teachers held in Rome. Despite attempts to control public instruction in depth, fascism failed to erode the strong position of the Catholic Church in the field of education: Catholicism, in fact, was able to voice its point of view in the Enciclopedia Italiana *itself.*

Several figures of the antifascist movement: above, from the left, Lorenzo Da Bove, Filippo Turati, Carlo Rosselli, Sandro Pertini, and Ferruccio Parri a Calvi, in Corsica, during Turati's flight from Italy in 1926.
Below, again from the left, Cesare Pavese, Leone Ginzburg, Franco Antonicelli and editor Frassinelli in the Langhe.

enjoyed little more than an expansive sea of indifference that surrounded islands of loyal followers on the one hand, and those of real opponents on the other. This moral climate of indifference and resignation, of outward conformism and private skepticism that has been common to other modern dictatorships, also constituted a formidable barrier to the strengthening and maintenance of the political traditions of the party's adversaries. Antifascism undoubtedly had idealistic roots that were diffuse and spread to all parts of Italy, and none of its movements was ever entirely quieted by the regime. But the impact of the political defeat suffered between 1922 and 1925, which was embittered by internal clashes that tore the antifascists to pieces, prevented antifascism from coming together as a unified movement throughout most of the 1920s.

Notwithstanding this fundamental limitation, one could not explain the history of fascism without also understanding that of antifascism, its complement. This is a very important historical distinction that sets the Italian experience apart from that of Germany under Hitler, or that of Japan during the same period. The presence, though meager or divided, of antifascist elements throughout the whole course of the dictatorship, helps to explain the nature and characteristics of the Resistance between 1943 and 1945, as well as during the successive historical periods, which witnessed Italy's rebirth as a free and democratic republic.

If, between the years 1921 and 1925, no antifascist party was exempt from responsibility for the lack of political resistance against the fascists, some were certainly more guilty than others.

The various liberal groups, including the Liberal Party, which assumed its name in 1922, precisely when the liberal State began its descent from power, were destroyed by the attraction that fascism exerted on forces of the right. Pro-Mussolini elements among the liberals had a propensity to support the turn toward authoritarianism. Thus, old Giolitti eschewed openly antifascist pronouncements; Salandra was considered an honorary fascist by Mussolini; it was only Nitti who opted for exile in Paris. The Liberal-Democrats, prepared for a concrete political battle against the fascists, constituted a slim minority, and met with increased harassment: personalities as different as Giovanni Amendola and Piero Gobetti suffered numerous physical assaults from *squadristi*, and were forced to take refuge in France, where they later died.

In 1924, after an initial attitude of benevolence toward the national government, conservative liberalism, personified in the philosopher and historian

THE INDIFFERENT AND THE ANTIFASCISTS

The title of Alberto Moravia's celebrated first novel, *Gli indifferenti* (The Indifferent), published in 1929, might be adopted, from a historic perspective, to describe the vast gray area lying between fascism and antifascism. In fact, a large portion of the Italian population that remained at the margins of genuine involvement in fascist organizations never nurtured either a generic antifascist sentiment, nor one of active political opposition. This mass of the indifferent could be characterized as conformist, passive, and irresponsible in the face of the regime. This profound moral apathy and lack of civic "upbringing" registered by so many literary and artistic documents is one of the most serious and long-lasting bequests of fascism to the national character, and to the identity of the Italian people in the twentieth century. On the other hand, one characteristic that distinguishes fascism from Nazism is the presence, throughout the *Ventennio* (the twenty years), of an opposition to the dictatorship. While isolated, defeated or divided within, the antifascists were active in emigration-related and clandestine activities, and in fact maintained connections with the young people who undertook their long voyage through fascism (paraphrasing the title of a celebrated book by Ruggero Zangrandi), but ultimately became the Resistance.

The liberals Nitti and Croce, the Catholics Sturzo and Ferrari, the democrats Salvemini and Sforza, the socialists Turati and Nenni, the communists Togliatti and Longo, are among the protagonists in this long struggle. The list of victims of fascist violence, from liberals to communists, includes Gobetti and Giovanni Amendola, Don Minzoni and Matteotti, the Rosselli brothers, and Gramsci. To these illustrious names are added thousands of individuals condemned to prison only because of their ideas, which in fascist Italy were crimes. ■

It would be impossible to tell fascism's story without telling that of antifascism, its complement. This very important historical distinction differentiates, at least in part, the Italian experience from that of Germany or Japan.

Benedetto Croce, was the example — unique rather than rare — of the persistence of a cultural tradition of antifascism that did not bend before the Mussolini dictatorship, although it did suffer ostracism by the regime. Nevertheless, it failed to undertake a critical analysis of the artifice of pre-fascist liberalism, which had opened the door to the capitulation of the democracy.

Other more isolated personalities, like Luigi Einaudi (and his son Giulio, founder of the publishing house of the same name in 1933), Giustino Fortunato, Umberto Zanotti Bianco, and Guido Dorso strove to maintain institutions, journals, and traditional areas of study such as economic problems and southern Italian thought, which constituted oases at the margins of the academic culture, which had generally aligned itself with fascism.

In the Catholic world, the Conciliation dug an even

deeper trench between a pro-fascist or benevolently neutral majority and the small number of antifascists surviving the experience of the Popular Party. Don Luigi Sturzo had been one of the first antifascists forced into exile in 1924; he was distanced from Italy more by pressures from the Vatican than by direct fascist violence. Giuseppe Donati and Francesco Luigi Ferrari found asylum in Paris, while Alcide De Gasperi retired, finding modest employment in the Vatican Library.

Although badly weakened by defections that had swelled the ranks of the fascists, republicans and socialists, the anarchists and communists constituted the whips of opposition to the dictatorship. Among republicans, Eugenuio Chiesa and Fernando Schiavetti emigrated to France, while Mario Angeloni and Randolfo Pacciardi actively combated fascism in the Spanish Civil War.

After having lived through the split within the Communist Party (1921), the unitary socialists subsequently divided again in 1922, but reunited in 1930. To the reformist movement of the PSI belonged a number of historical leaders who were forced into exile: Filippo Turati, Claudio Treves, Giuseppe Emanuele Modigliani, Bruno Buozzi, and the younger of the Rosselli brothers, Carlo. Among the mainline socialists, activist leader Pietro Nenni assumed the guiding role, while other socialist exponents, including Sandro Pertini and intellectuals Lelio Basso and Rodolfo Morandi, suffered the squalor of Italian fascist prisons.

Among the disunited ranks of the anarchists, were the outlaws Armando Borghi and Camillo Berneri. Fundamentalist militants crowded the prison cells, and included Michele Schirru, Domenico Bovone, and Angelo Sbardellotto, who were shot after being condemned by the Special Tribunal.

The greatest burden of repression was borne by the communists. In 1926 the entire directorate of the PCI

A membership card of the "Antifascist Concentration," a movement formed by Italian antifascists in exile in France in 1927. The Concentration brought together Republicans, Socialists, members of the General Confederation of Work, and the League for the Rights of man. Left, the Republican Randolfo Pacciardi during the Spanish Civil War.

*P*age one of the newspaper,
Justice and Liberty, *announces
the assassination, in France, of
Carlo and Nello Rosselli. The two
brothers, forces behind a
movement that brought together
Emilio Lussu, Aldo Garosci, Leone
Ginzburg, and Gaetano
Salvemini, among others, were
killed by a special fascist squad in
June 1937.*

was cut off from the party. Antonio Gramsci, Umberto Terracini, Mauro Scoccimarro, and Giovanni Roveda were condemned to extremely long sentences in prison. Palmiro Togliatti succeeded in creating, in France, a foreign party center, and, in Moscow a school for militants who would re-enter Italy clandestinely.

While the first party secretary, Amadeo Bordiga, was marginalized, under the leadership of Togliatti the party was made to suffer the violence of a fascist dictatorship, as well as tragic directives received from Moscow. Stalinism was at this time marked by a struggle against "social-fascism." This placed the socialists on the same plane of enmity as the fascists: only in 1934 was it possible to reestablish relations between communists and socialists, with the "unity of action" pact. Angelo Tasca, Ruggero Grieco, Giuseppe Di Vittorio, Luigi Longo, Pietro Secchia, and Giancarlo Pajetta participated in Paris and in Italy in the not always easy elaboration of a political strategy aimed at effectively combating the regime.

This strategy undoubtedly produced some success, and it was thanks to a new generation of opponents who were ready to risk all, enter into the fascist mass organizations themselves and voice propaganda against the regime that the PCI gained support. In some regions and localities in Italy, communism's key to success was its almost complete identification as an active, antifascist presence.

The majority of those condemned by the Special Tribunal were communists, as were thousands of opponents of the regime who were forced into police confinement (a fascist version of forced domicile far from one's true place of residence), or subjected to any number of intermediate repressive or preventive measures imposed by the dictatorship, such as temporary imprisonment, warnings, inclusion in the "album" of subversives, or the criminal file of suspected antifascists.

We consider, finally, the Justice and Liberty movement, founded in 1929, which represented the greatest innovation of antifascism in Italy. This movement distinguished itself from the communists, as well as from the antifascist Coalition formed in 1927 in Paris of the two Socialist parties — the Republicans (the Confederation of Work), and the Italian League for the Rights of Man. Under the leadership of Carlo Rosselli, Justice and Liberty utilized the talents of militants that had emigrated, as well as those in Italy: Emilio Lussu, Gaetano Salvemini, Riccardo Bauer, Ernesto Rossi, Aldo Garosci, Franco Venturi, Augusto Monti, Vittorio Foa, and Leone Ginzburg. The liberal-socialists Aldo Capitani and Guido Calogero were particularly active in formulating a fundamental critique of the pre-fascist political experience, which, they argued, should have fostered the development of a "third force" that was both democratic and progressive from the classical bases of liberalism, socialism and communism.

The regime understood early on the importance of the challenge that these new and more active antifascist groups were launching. In 1937, the same year in which French assassins, hired by the Italian secret service, assassinated Carlo and Nello Rosselli, Antonio Gramsci succumbed to the extreme conditions of fascist prisons. An original interpreter of twentieth-century Marxism and a personality inspired by a rich and complex critical conception of political engagement based on the study of social and human reliability, Gramsci left a legacy of works destined to renew and redeem not only the culture, but also the international public image of the "real country" that fascism had caged and disfigured, but not yet removed from the world of contemporary peoples, or the community of civilized nations.

A photo of Antonio Gramsci in the identification list maintained by the Italian police. Among the founders of the Italian Communist Party in 1921, Gramsci (1891–1937) was condemned in 1928 by the Special Tribunal to twenty years in prison, which did irremediable damage to his health.

Chapter 6

FOREIGN
POLICY

FROM 1923, WHEN MUSSOLINI ORDERED THE OCCUPATION OF THE GREEK ISLAND OF CORFU, IT BECAME CLEAR THAT ONE OF FASCISM'S PRINCIPAL OBJECTIVES WAS TO UPSET THE EUROPEAN ORDER THAT HAD EMERGED AFTER THE FIRST WORLD WAR AND THE TREATY OF VERSAILLES.

An inflamed nationalism and an avenging imperialism: these were the two first inspirations of fascism. To put such assertions into practice had limitations and was a daunting task.

While the Mussolini government, from its formation in 1922 until 1929, was able to enter a stable international economic and diplomatic context favorable to the early establishment of fascism, this same context did not permit a great deal of activity in the foreign policy arena. Italy could still enjoy the position of victorious power, even though fascists had denounced the "mutilated victory" and the "conciliatory" character of liberal diplomacy. Mussolini breathed a new dynamism into Italian foreign policy that made it clear that the presumption of danger associated with foreign adventures — which were denounced by antifascists — were not entirely unfounded.

Initially, the old conservative establishment exercised a counterweight to Mussolini's wildly ambitious programs. This was especially true during the tenure, until 1926, of secretary general for foreign affairs Salvatore Contarini. Subsequently, however, several fascist bosses, including Dino Grandi, entered the interim ministry. Grandi held the title of foreign minister from 1929 to 1932. During that same period, fascist organizations abroad began to dif-

Adolf Hitler, German Chancellor as of January 1933, and Mussolini in Venice, June 1934. Initially, relations with Hitler's Germany were not the most cordial, but as of 1936, with the war in Ethiopia and the subsequent break with the Western powers, the ties of Italian fascism to Hitler's Germany strengthened.

*August 1923: an Italian
expeditionary corps occupies the
island of Corfu after a heavy
bombardment. The operation
was organized by Mussolini in
response to the August 27 attack
against an Italian military mission
in Greece. The occupation of the
island, which lasted through
September, was the first Italian
act to challenge the balance that
had been established after the
Great War and formation of the
League of Nations.*

fuse propaganda materials and perform related activities
outside of official channels; and numerous cultural institutions — those designated to address problems relating
to Italian emigration throughout the world — were continually forced to take on the job of strongly asserting presumed Italian rights to territory and peoples, as well as
the equally presumed primacy of the Italian civilization.

Destabilizing Europe

Mussolini was inclined to use unorthodox methods,
including secret diplomatic action and financing overseas
pro-fascist newspapers and journalists, as well as terrorist
movements, to discredit and weaken other nations, such
as the newly formed Yugoslavia, with which the fascists
refused to establish friendly relations.

Thus, in 1923, the attack in Corfu against an Italian
military mission provoked the extremist order to occupy
the Greek island — a response that was intentionally dis-
proportionate, in order to make clear to the other powers,
and in particular, to the League of Nations, that the fascist
government would act according to a logic based on the
defense of its own self-interests, and the affirmation of
Italy's autonomy as a great power.

Furthermore, throughout the 1920s, fascist foreign policy pursued an attitude of hidden hostility in its relations with France, the nation that gave refuge to Italian antifascists, and looked after the small democratic powers that had emerged in central, eastern and southern Europe after the collapse of the German, Hapsburg, Tsarist, and Ottoman empires. The Italian regime was, on the other hand, benevolently protected by its traditional friendship with Great Britain, and buffered by new financial support provided by American capital.

The postwar arrangement in Europe was, after all, rigidly based on the peace treaties of 1919, which Mussolini could not openly renounce. Moreover, beginning in the early 1930s, the fascist government was burdened by the difficult and draining re-conquest of Libya. The control of this colony, which Italy had acquired in 1912, had been effectively lost during the years before the First World War, with the exception of certain coastal bridgeheads.

In the Libyan hinterland, the Italian political and military authorities (from Giuseppe Volpi to Emilio De Bono, from Pietro Badoglio to Rodolfo Graziani) fought fiercely against the resistance of the indigenous guerrillas, as well as the Arab nomad population, which had sided with the

Marshal Rodolfo Graziani (1882–1955) in 1931, when he was the Italian governor of Libya. During the First World War, the Italian-occupied positions in the colony had been reduced to the coastal strip; fascism took it upon itself to re-conquer the Libyan hinterland, employing harsh techniques against the guerrillas until, in 1931, Omar el Mukhtar, the soul of Libyan resistance, was captured and hanged.

During the late 1920s, Mussolini began to work toward the objective of revising the peace treaties in order to grant Italy more favorable status both in colonial lands and in Europe.

rebels. These adventures provided opportunities for experimentation with methods that would be more generally applied in later years: concentration camps, torture and reprisal, farcical military trials, summary executions, and acts of racism that were typically fascist. In this way they distinguished themselves from the methods of classical colonialism.

Mussolini was intolerant of the pacifist ideology that was being promoted by the League of Nations, dissatisfied by the long disarmament negotiations that did not treat all the allies (in particular, Italy and France) equally, and anxious to obtain results that were more spectacular than those of the reparation accords and the war debt plans (of Dawes in 1924, and Young in 1929) or the Locarno Pact of 1925. Therefore he began, during the second half of the 1920s, to work toward the ultimate goal of revising those treaties in order to grant Italy more favorable status both in Europe and the colonies. At the same time, the traditional Balkan-Danube directive governing Italian foreign policy was reinstated to contain the revisionism of defeated powers like Hungary — main-

tained, in fact, by a reactionary regime — against Yugoslavia and Romania. A true Italian protectorate was established over Albania, and a sort of exclusive stewardship was established with regard to Austria, whose regime was moving continually more to the right, and assuming a fascist identity of its own.

Other groups and paramilitary formations of the extreme right were maintained by fascist emissaries and by the Italian secret services: Ante Pavelic, the head of the Croatian separatist terrorists, was protected by Mussolini and given a haven in Italy; the Macedonian terrorists were similarly subsidized in order that they might wreak havoc and raise pretexts that would set the stage for Italian foreign policy to cast its line in those murky waters. When all was said and done, Italy was seen to be taking the place of France as the point of reference in a new Danube/Balkan order. For example, the terrorists who, in 1934, assassinated King Alexander of Yugoslavia, and also the French Minister Barthou in Marseilles, had embarked from bases in Italy.

Mussolini with Foreign Minister Dino Grandi (on the right), German Chancellor Bruning (facing), and German Foreign Minister Curtius (his back to the viewer) in a photograph taken by Erich Solomon at the Hotel Excelsior in Rome, during a meeting between Italy and Germany in 1931.
Left, Mussolini celebrates the "fascist conscription" of 1927 in Rome, receiving the salutes of the militia recruits.

The Conquest of Empire

Even during this phase the policy of the regime was not entirely "pacific," as those seeking to contrast it with the later phases of uninterrupted conflict have sought to argue. The continuity of Mussolini's actions lay precisely in their underlying ideological inspiration. Thus, after the trauma of the world economic crisis, when internal stability became questionable because of runaway unemployment and a dearth of consumables, fascism unleashed all of the aggressive potential that its logic of violence permitted. The regime shifted its obsessive and by now mandatory search for success — as is often the case for dictatorships — to overseas battlegrounds. It could no longer maintain itself by means of internally generated propaganda alone. To elevate the degree of tension, and thereby maintain the interest of the masses who

*Haile Selassie (1892–1975),
Emperor of Ethiopia. In 1923,
Ethiopia, the last independent
African state, was admitted to the
League of Nations, and in 1928
Haile Selassie negotiated a treaty
of friendship with Italy.
Nevertheless by 1932 Mussolini
began preparations for a possible
attack against Ethiopia from
Italian bases in Eritrea and
Somalia.
Right, a contingent of industrial
workers departs for Somalia, with
the offensive against Ethiopia
imminent.*

were anticipating ever more grandiose mirages, Mussolini decided on a sure-to-be rancorous course: the conquest of Ethiopia.

Ethiopia was the last African region that was "available" for annexation by a European colonial power, but it was also the only African state that was independent, and a member of the League of Nations. The undertaking was therefore likely to be fraught with political and diplomatic difficulties, of which Mussolini was certainly cognizant. As early as 1932, with the invasion imminent, he had given preliminary dispositions to the Italian colonial authorities in Eritrea and Somalia, and in 1934, addressed a detailed memo to the military forces that set as the objective of the military expedition the "total conquest of Ethiopia."

Late in 1934, an incident along the Somali/Ethiopian border, near Ual-Ual, provided the regime with an excuse to denounce imagined threats of aggression by Ethiopia against the Italian colony. It was, by now, clear that Mussolini was searching for a pretext for invasion. In early 1935, a meeting with French foreign minister Laval convinced him that he would have a free hand in Ethiopia, and the subsequent Stresa conference confirmed that not even England would block the fascist enterprise. Throughout the year, the large numbers of troops and transport vehicles that were being sent from Italian ports to Eritrea made it clear to all observers that war was imminent.

On October 3, 1935, Italian troops crossed the Ethiopian border, performing an act of aggression that took place with no prior warning, and in the absence of a declaration of war. Ethiopian leader Haile Selassie made

The directives and plans of action to resolve the Italo-Ethiopian question, presented by Mussolini to the armed forces on December 30, 1934, are drastic: "The problem of Italo-Ethiopian relations has been relocated [...] to a different plane: what was a problem of diplomacy has become one of force: a "historic" problem that must be resolved by the only means with which such problems have always been resolved — the use of arms [...]. Taking account of previous events, it is necessary that we conclude, logically, that time works against us: the longer we take to dispose of the problem, the more difficult the task will become, and greater the sacrifice. The second and equally logical conclusion is: it is necessary to resolve the problem as soon as possible, as soon as our military preparations give us the certainty of victory [...] Once definitively decided on, the objective of this war can be none other than the destruction of the Ethiopian armed forces and the total conquest of Ethiopia. The empire cannot be built in any other way.

In order for our armies' victories to be swift and absolute, it will be necessary to employ our mechanized forces — forces which the Ethiopians do not yet possess, but which they might have within a few years on a grand scale [...]. Aside from the 60,000 troops already in the country, it will be necessary to deploy an equal number of home forces. It will be necessary to concentrate at least 250 airplanes in Eritrea and 50 in Somalia, 150 tanks in Eritrea and 50 in Somalia. Absolute superiority in artillery and gas, an abundance of munitions, the 60,000 — still better, 100,000 — soldiers from the homeland must be ready in Eritrea by October 1935 [...]. After the Japanese manner, there will be no need to officially declare war, and in any case we will insist on the purely defensive nature of the operations.

No worries from the domestic point of view: among the fascist masses, the conviction of the inevitability of the attack , as well as the conviction that if we were to wait the operation would become more arduous, have become quite diffuse. Among our youth, the tone is even more intense. Some old-timers fear this "adventure," because they believe the war would be fought with old systems, but they are wrong, and moreover they carry no political or social weight. This is a problem that has existed since 1885. Ethiopia is the last strip of Africa without European owners. The Gordian knot of Italo-Ethiopian relations will become ever more entangled. We must cut it before it is too late!" ■

an appeal to the League of Nations, which could not, given the clear violation of its statute, fail to act by condemning this aggression against a member state. On November 18, the League imposed economic sanctions against Italy, but excluded oil — the raw material that was indispensable for the conduct of any modern military campaign — from the embargo.

This incomplete economic embargo, the diplomatic vacillation of the western powers, and the failure to participate in the embargo by states that were not members of the League (like the United States), favored Italy. Mussolini, in fact, was able to mobilize nationalist pride on this occasion, and responded by placing counter-sanctions on

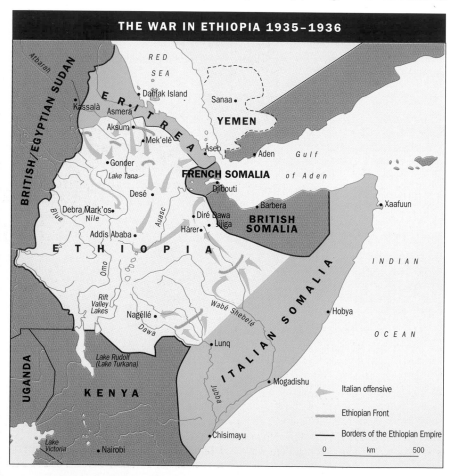

THE WAR IN ETHIOPIA 1935–1936

Italian offensive
Ethiopian Front
Borders of the Ethiopian Empire

0   km   500

products and merchandise coming from those countries that had launched the "odious economic sanctions" against Italy. Italy, Mussolini maintained, was doing nothing more than bringing modern Christian civilization to the African nation. All Italian wives followed the example of Queen Elena by donating their wedding rings to the fatherland; the parish priests organized a vast network of propaganda and moral support to maintain morale on the home front.

The war, in itself, presented no surprises, since the Ethiopians were often armed with outdated guns, guns that had been captured from the Italians at the time of the defeat inflicted by Melenik on troops sent to Africa by Crispi in 1896. Mussolini had put half a million men in the field, including draftees, blackshirt volunteers from militia units and engineers. An entire battery of modern weapons was being used against the Ethiopian army, as well as against semi-deserted villages and defenseless civilian populations. These included aerial bombardments and the "carpet" use of toxic gases, which had been outlawed by international conventions. A number of fascist leaders participated in sadistic summary executions and torture of the Ethipians.

Italian troops from the Somali and Eritrean fronts meet at Diredaua. Launched in October 1935, and entrusted to Graziani and De Bono, the offensive against Ethiopia was concluded at the beginning of May 1936, with the entry of Italian troops into Addis Ababa.

Under the guidance of Badoglio, Italian troops opened the final offensive and entered Addis Ababa in early May 1936. The demonstrations organized in Italy by the regime signaled the apogee of fascist popularity: Mussolini was able to proclaim the return of the Empire to "the fated hills of Rome," and the king assumed the title of Emperor of Ethiopia.

The ensuing diplomatic break with the western powers, and in particular with English and French public opinion, which had grown progressively antifascist, placed Italy in an isolated position which, in the long run, was unsustainable, and led to the rapprochement with Nazi Germany.

The Alliance with Germany

During the course of the war with Ethiopia, Hitler — who had gained power in 1933 and by 1934 was a deferential guest of Mussolini — offered German coal to Italy to replace the supply that was to have come from England but had been suspended by sanctions. Moreover, Nazi Germany was seeking to regain full possession of the Rhineland and remilitarize it without intervention by the western powers. Such remilitarization constituted an explicit violation of the 1919 peace treaty. Germany took advantage of the fact that fascist Italy was keeping England and France occupied in the international tangle of the war in Ethiopia — the first real challenge to postwar equilibrium and a harbinger of the Second World War.

Notwithstanding some reciprocal diffidence and minor differences in national objectives, the two principal fascist regimes prepared to travel on parallel tracks in what was no longer simply a foreign policy, but rather, an increasingly violent challenge to peace, a predisposition to assault world power and a proclamation of permanent "near-war."

During the summer of 1936, Mussolini had his son-in-law, Galeazzo Ciano, named to the foreign ministry (Ciano had been undersecretary, and then minister of press and propaganda). In the autumn, the first accords of Italian-German cooperation were established. *Il Duce* described these accords as an indestructible "Rome-Berlin Axis." In 1937, fascist Italy left the League of Nations and joined Germany and Japan in an anticommunist alliance, the Anti-Comintern Pact.

The joint Italian-German action taken during the course of the Spanish Civil War was, as we shall see, decisive in solidifying an alliance that would later be cemented by diplo-

Galeazzo Ciano in command of the aerial squadron "Desperate," during military operations in Ethiopia in 1936. Mussolini's son-in-law, undersecretary and later minister of propaganda, Galeazzo Ciano, was named foreign minister during the summer of 1936.

matic collaboration in the Munich conference of 1938. But the unequivocal sign of ideological convergence between these two fascist powers was marked by the passage of the Racial Laws in Italy in 1938. Anti-Semitism did not then constitute one of the fundamental elements of Italian fascist ideology. To be sure, numerous incidents of racist acts performed by Italians had surfaced in Libya and in Ethiopia: in 1936, in fact, in the East African Empire, a highly discriminatory law against indigenous subjects was passed. But until then, Italian Jews within Italy had only been the victims of invectives by low-level fascist "intellectuals."

In contempt of a community that, since the *Risorgimento*, had integrated itself well into the fabric of the nation — producing illustrious personalities in both the world of culture and the world of business — the regime showed various signs of imitating the Nazis. In the summer of 1938 a document was published by "scientists" (university professors, doctors, anthropologists, and zoologists), that for the first time certified the existence of disparities between races. Then the magazine *La difesa della razza* (The Defense of the Race) came into existence — a journal that was directly inspired by the PNF. Finally, the government denied the right of foreign Jews to reside in Italy; it denied Jewish Italians access to the teaching profession (at any level), and it revoked the right of

Italy signs the Anti-Comintern Pact on November 6, 1937, in Rome. Japanese ambassador Hotta, Galeazzo Ciano and German Foreign Minister Ribbentrop pose for the camera. The alliance with Japan and Germany marked a foreign policy realignment for Italy after the crisis with France and Britain provoked by the Ethiopian expedition.

Jewish students to attend secondary schools. Then, in the autumn, a number of new legal provisions were issued that banned marriages between Italians of the Aryan race and people of other races, blocked Jewish entry into military service, as well as other public administrative offices, and placed strong limits on the freedom of Jews to practice the buying and selling of real estate, engage in professional activities, and manage businesses.

These racial laws did not lead to violent forms of segregation for a number of reasons: the typical lethargy of

The rapport with Nazi Germany was also a "brutal friendship." In his dealings with Mussolini, Hitler showed himself to be the stronger character of the two: he was more open to playing a game of chance, and in choosing the proper time for a diplomatic initiative.

the Italian bureaucracy, the broad discretion that was permitted in the application of the laws, and, in the end, the scant public enthusiasm with which the laws were greeted. Nonetheless, among some of the more fanatic fascists, in certain institutions and official magazines, and within those levels of society that were most open to prejudice, an anti-Semitic pseudo-culture did take hold. One of the few enduring Italian traits — racial tolerance — was, for the first time, being seriously eroded by fascism. From this point in time fascism added the racist element to its ideological baggage, and it is a trait that, unfortunately, has been transferred by means of neo-fascist movements to our own times. There was some repulsive truth in Mussolini's words to Ciano, when he observed: "Now that the Italians have been inoculated with anti-Semitism, it will continue to circulate and develop on its own."

The War in Spain

One of the peculiar characteristics of fascist violence — used against both internal and foreign foes — was to establish conditions of military, technological and political superiority, and then operate from the position of a bully who speaks loudly toward the weak. Used against small nations and ethnic minorities, this policy reaped success at little cost. But the international position of Italy during the fascist period, notwithstanding Mussolini's arrogance and propaganda talents, failed to change as a consequence. Because of its relatively low level of economic preparedness, and the questionable quality of its armaments, Italy remained forever last among the great powers, or perhaps more appropriately, first among the second-tier states.

Moreover, an international partnership with a truly dominant great power has always been a necessity for Italy, dating from the time of the *Risorgimento* and unification. France in 1859, Germany in 1866, the Entente (France, England, the United States) during the First World War, and then Germany once more after the economic crisis of 1929–1932, have been Italy's allies.

The rapport with Nazi Germany was certainly what may be termed a "brutal friendship" because of the disparity of forces. But the bond of ideological solidarity helped to

Mussolini at a gathering of 10,000 war volunteers in the mid-1930s. For the occasion, Mussolini wore the uniform of supreme head of the militia. During the course of the 1930s, Mussolini's public appearances became less frequent.
Left, a military parade held in Mussolini's presence (1937).

Colonial troops of the army against Spain embark in German planes, July 1936. The success of the military action against the Spanish Republic was made possible by the air bridge organized between Africa and Spain using Italian and German aircraft. This was the first time in which fascism and Nazism collaborated directly for military purposes.

silence other differences that were based on contrasting national interests. In his interactions with Mussolini, Hitler showed himself to be the more controlling of the two. Hitler was more open to playing a game of chance, and choosing the proper time for a diplomatic, as opposed to a military initiative: the student had by this time surpassed the master. A certain equality in rank between the two dictators was maintained, however, over the course of the Spanish Civil War.

In July 1936, General Francisco Franco and other military officers initiated an insurrection against the legitimate Spanish government. Mussolini and Ciano were ready to support Franco's nationalists with shipments of arms and a corps of volunteers, which eventually came to include tens of thousands of regular troops. Hitler offered only a corps of aviators (the Condor Legion), with limited means but advanced technology, which made a reputation for itself through its bombardments of cities and localities under the control of the Spanish Republican government. The Spanish Republic had been isolated as a result of the hypocritical non-interventionist policies of the French and British democracies, while the vital support by Italian and German forces to Franco's army continued.

The civil war came to an end early in 1939, though not without the international antifascist brigades having inflicted major defeats on the fascist troops. (In the 1937 battle of Guadalajara, for example, Italian antifascist volunteers defeated units of Mussolini's black shirts.)

The war in Spain, which followed the campaign in Ethiopia without a pause, contributed to an impoverishment of Italian military potential. Unlike the African enterprise, which had aroused so much enthusiasm, the anticommunist *cruzada* of 1936–39 showed the first signs of cracks in the edifice of the reactionary regime by bringing forth doubts and planting seeds of skepticism and uncertainty, in particular, among young people.

The creation in 1937 of a single, militarily centralized organization, the *Gioventù italiana dell Littorio* (GIL, or Italian Youth of the Littorio — the littorio being the fascist symbol, which was inherited from the Romans); the obligatory Roman salute, instead of the handshake; the abolition of "Lei" in favor of "Voi"; the forced and often comical Italianization of foreign names (Grand Hotel became Grand'Albergo, but more bizarre were additions such as "in pied'uomo," which replaced "barman"); and the worrisome racial laws were all associated with the accelera-

Italian armored vehicles in Guadalajara in 1939, during the parade to celebrate the fall of the city into the hands of the nationalists. Earlier, during the battle of Guadalajara in March 1937, the Italian (fascist) contingent was defeated by Italian antifascist volunteers who had been organized into international brigades.

The logic of totalitarianism pushed Mussolini increasingly into the arms of Hitler; a rapprochement with France and England would have led, sooner or later, to a mitigation of the characteristics of the fascist state.

tion of totalitarian tendencies. It became clear that these new policies and organizations would be critical in sustaining the preparation for the great European war that was to be undertaken in the fascist conquest of "vital space." But the bellicose climate created by the regime's propaganda against hated France and "perfidious Albion" evoked clear concern among those who were beginning to calculate the eventual price of a duel to the death.

The German ally, in any case, obtained all or most of the spoils of the aggression that had been threatened in collaboration with Italy. In 1938, Hitler would realize one of his oldest dreams with the annexation of Austria; in the same year, through the Munich accords, he would secure, essentially, the capitulation of the Western powers, as they consented to the dismemberment of Bohemia and Slovakia, and the assignment of a Sudetenland protectorate to Germany. Then in March 1939, notwithstanding the Munich accords, Nazi troops entered Prague and annexed all of Czechoslovakia. Europe's geography was changing rapidly, and no response from France or England was forthcoming.

THE FORCES OF FASCISM

The numerical composition of the major associations created by fascism to mold a consensus as they stood in 1939, on the eve of the Second World War:

THE NATIONAL FASCIST PARTY

Fascist Combat Units	2,633,514
University Fascist Groups	105,883
Italian Youth of the Littorio (Italian Fascist Youth)	
Sons of the Wolf (6–8 years)	1,546,389
Balilla (8–12 years)	1,746,560
Little Italians (girls 8–12)	1,622,766
The Vanguard (12–18)	906,785
Young Italians (girls 12–18)	441,254
Young fascists (18–21)	1,176,798
Young fascists (female)	450,995
Fascist women	774,181
Rural workers	1,481,321
Home workers (female)	501,415

SCHOOL ASSOCIATIONS

Elementary schools	121,437
Middle Schools	40,896
University professors	3,272
University assistants	2,468
Fine arts and libraries	2,500

OTHER ASSOCIATIONS

Public employment	294,265
Railroad workers	137,902
Mail and telegraph workers	83,184
State industrial workers	120,205
National union of retired military officers	259,865
National after-work recreational organization	3,832,248
Olympic Committee	809,659
Italian Naval League	198,522
Army units	1,309,600

In Munich, Mussolini had acted as mediator between the western powers and Germany, returning home acclaimed as "the savior of peace." But this was a role that was uncomfortable for *il Duce*, and one that placed him at a dead end. The logic of totalitarianism pushed him increasingly into the arms of Hitler, while an eventual rapprochement with France and England would have led, sooner or later, to a mitigation of the characteristics of the fascist state.

The dilemma of choosing between war and peace would, in essence, be resolved by choosing between the reactionary imperialist camp and that of the democracies — a choice which Italian fascism had, in reality, already made simply by its own nature.

In May of 1937 the first anniversary of the Ethiopian conquest is celebrated with a military parade along the via dei Fori imperiali. *Notwithstanding the fact that propaganda emphasized Italy's military potential, the Italian army on the eve of the Second World War remained seriously underprepared.*

Chapter 7

THE CATASTROPHE
OF WAR

On June 10, 1940, as the Germans advanced past the Rhine and through the Ardennes, Mussolini declared war against France and Great Britain. From that moment on, an unprepared army would suffer one defeat after another, and the paths followed by the regime and the Italian nation would diverge inexorably.

In response to the German annexation of Czechoslovakia, Mussolini and Ciano undertook to conquer and occupy Albania in April 1939, with King Victor Emmanuel III adding the Albanian crown to his headgear. This was the last action in which the Fascists showed themselves capable of keeping up with the Nazis, whose capacity for rearmament was far superior to that of the Italians.

On May 22, 1939, the Italian-German entente culminated in the signing of a true military alliance containing a clause that was previously unknown to the annals of international relations: wherever, and under whatever circumstances one of the two co-signers found itself embroiled in conflict (even in an offensive operation unleashed by itself, and not simply a classic case of aggression suffered at the hands of another), the ally would immediately come to its aid. The fascist leaders congratulated themselves by defining this alliance as the Pact of Steel, an irrevocable step forward, a formidable threat against their enemies. Ciano wrote in his diary that the military pact was "pure dynamite," fooling himself into believing that such a deterrent would bring down the remaining defenses of those western democracies that had been slandered by fascist propaganda as plutocratic, Masonic and controlled by Jews.

Italian soldiers depart on the expeditionary force to Russia in June 1941. Sent to the eastern front without adequate equipment, they met with a bloody defeat.

Italian troops disembark at the port of Valona, Albania, in April 1939. The Albanian occupation, which was hastily decided upon in response to the German occupation of Czechoslovakia, was fascism's last step on the path to European war.
Right: On May 22, 1939, Ciano and Hitler sign the Pact of Steel in Berlin.

Italy Enters the War

Mussolini's timetable for entering the war did not coincide with that of Hitler, who was in a much greater hurry. Nevertheless, during the summit of 1939, the moment arrived: after repeated threats, the Nazis invaded Poland on September 3. The Poles requested aid from their allies, and France and England declared war against Germany. Caught off guard by the fast-moving events, and not given prior notice of the attack by Hitler, Mussolini and Ciano arrived at a formula of non-belligerence: they would abstain momentarily from intervening. As the term suggests, it was not a question of moving in a pacifist direction, or of setting a new course in the direction of stable neutrality; rather, it was merely a suspension of Italy's entry into war.

In a sense, this was the last of Mussolini's realistic decisions. He was well aware of Italy's lack of military preparedness (according to his calculations, Italy would not have been properly equipped until 1942–43), but he was also vigilant, and anxious not to miss any occasion to profit from his share of the booty lying in Hitler's wake. However, Italian policy was highly contradictory, and dependent on the need to secure precious foreign currency through (for example) the sale of arms to France and Yugoslavia — this during a period when the nation should have been readying itself to attack these countries. The dependence on foreign energy, the debilitating loans, and the depletion of the Bank of Italy's gold reserves, rendered fascist Italy highly vulnerable: she

THE PACT OF STEEL

On May 22, 1939, Italy and Germany signed the friendship and alliance pact. "H.M. the King of Italy and Albania and Emperor of Ethiopia, and the Chancellor of the German Reich affirm that the moment has arrived to solidify [...] the tight ties of friendship and solidarity that exist between Fascist Italy and National Socialist Germany [...].

"The peoples of Italy and Germany, bound together by the deep affinity of their conceptions of life and their complete solidarity of interests, have decided to proceed, in the future as well as the present, side by side, and with their forces united, to secure their vital space [...].

Art. 1. The contracting parties will keep in permanent contact with the aim of maintaining mutual understanding in all questions relating to their common interests, or the European situation in general.

Art. 2. Whenever the common interests of the contracting parties are jeopardized by international events of any kind, those parties will enter into consultation, without delay, on the measures to be taken that will best defend their interests. Whenever the security or other vital interests of one of the contracting parties should be threatened from the outside, the other contracting party will give to the threatened party its full political and diplomatic support, with the aim of eliminating this threat.

Art. 3. If despite the hopes and desires of the contracting parties it should happen that one of these might become involved in war-related activities with third or other parties, the other contracting party will come immediately to the aid of the contracting party that was initially engaged in conflict, supporting it with all of its military forces, by land, by sea, and in the air." ■

Italian colonial troops occupy a small fort in British Somaliland in June 1940, several days after the declaration of war.
Notwithstanding a number of early successes, the Ethiopian Empire was eventually crushed by the English counteroffensive: Addis Ababa fell as early as spring 1941.

had reserves of only three tons of petroleum per capita, as compared with 17,000 tons in the United States, 6,300 in the USSR, 3,810 in Germany, 3,700 in Great Britain, 227 in Japan, and 207 in France.

After the long autumn and winter months of the *drôle de guerre*, as it was aptly called in France — that phony war of positions on the Western Front — in spring of 1940, Nazi Germany initiated an impressive blitzkrieg, invading and conquering Norway, Denmark, Holland, and Belgium. By May, Hitler's armored divisions were overrunning France, and the French quickly became involved. Mussolini at this point argued that it was no longer possible to put off Italian intervention, and on June 10, 1940, declared war on France and England — with ammunition reserves for barely two months.

According to one version of the facts (probably inexact, but close to the truth), Mussolini is said to have commented during the early days of the conflict that it would cost him the deaths of several thousand Italian soldiers to sit as a victor at the peace talks. The aggression against France was, in any case, considered a vile and treacherous act by neutral powers such as the United States, which branded Mussolini's initiative, in the words of President Franklin Roosevelt, a "stab in the back."

It is a fact that Italy's changed position within the

opposing alliances of the Second World War represented the principal difference from the alignments of the previous war. Fascism had completely modified the internal and also the international positions of the country, which now found itself having to confront, as foes, the very same democratic nations of Europe and the western world to whose history and civic evolution Italy was once tightly bound, and from which it had greatly benefited.

This decision on the part of Mussolini was viewed by some scholars as evidence of the dictator's madness — he had become more and more a prisoner of his own megalomania. In fact, fascist Italy's entry into war was part of the logic that was consistent with all of the regime's policies, and fit well with its ultimate ends. Furthermore, *Il Duce*'s decision was shared, or at least not contested, by the dominant groups that had already given him their trust in 1922, in 1924, and in 1935. Without exception, no one among the fascist higher-ups — the monarchy and its court, the military leadership, or the capitalist magnates — ever revoked this one-man dictatorship's mandate to rule. The ruling economic and political class went along with Mussolini in forging its final attempt to measure up to its ambitions as a protagonist on the international stage. In spite of its relative weakness, Italian imperialism, through fascism, displayed all of its potential for danger. But an older pattern of conduct also emerged on this occasion — since the time of Italian unity the small Kingdom of Italy had to act as a participant in the major and minor conflicts of Europe.

The Illusion of a Brief War

Italian institutions and dominant social forces, as well as Mussolini and the fascist leadership, deluded themselves into thinking that the war would be brief. Further, they

King Victor Emmanuel III with Pietro Badoglio (1871–1956), commander of the Italian armed forces. Neither the court nor the military establishment opposed Italy's entry into war, which had been decided by Mussolini. The military leaders in particular, consistently avoided discussion of Italy's true war-time and productive capabilities.

Italy's entry into the Second World War followed logically from Italy's other aggressions: from the reconquest of Libya during the 1920s, to the invasion of Ethiopia, from the intervention in the Spanish Civil War, to the occupation of Albania in April 1939. On June 10, 1940, Mussolini said: "Combatants of the land, of the sea, of the air! Black shirts of the revolution and the legions! Men and women of Italy, of the Empire, and of the Kingdom of Albania! Listen! The hour of destiny is striking in the heavens of our fatherland. This is the hour of irrevocable decisions. The declaration of war has already been delivered to the ambassadors of Great Britain and France. Let us enter into the field opposed to the plutocratic and reactionary democracies of the West that, in every epoch, have blocked the progress, and frequently stifled the very existence of the Italian people.

"Several examples from the recent past may be summarized as follows: promises, threats, ransoms, and, in the end, the crowning of the edifice, the ignoble siege by 52 associated states [...]. Now all of this belongs to the past. If we, today, have decided to confront the risks and sacrifices of war, it is because our honor, our interests, and the future have imposed this decision with an iron will. A great people is really great only if it considers its obligations sacred, and if it does not evade the supreme trials that determine the course of history. We take arms to settle, after the problem of our continental borders, that of our maritime frontiers: we want to break the restraints imposed by the territorial and military order that suffocates us in our seas, since a nation of 45,000,000 souls is not really free if it has no access to the ocean [...].

"Italy, proletarian and fascist, is for the third time on its feet, strong, proud and solid as it has never been. The word for our times is but one, categorical and provocative: a word that already flies above and kindles hearts from the Alps to the Indian Ocean: Victory! And we will win and finally gain a lasting peace with justice for Italy, Europe and the World." ∎

could not conceive of assuming the role of an outside observer in this war, with their hands empty, without cynically having captured a part of its spoils. Nor did fascist propaganda impose limits on the objectives of Italian expansionism: Tunis, Malta, Gibraltar, Nice, Corsica, French and British Somaliland....

Beyond the presumption of the conflict's brevity, as well as the indispensability of the Kingdom's presence as an actor and later victor that would dictate the conditions of peace, another element dominated Mussolini's calculations. He had always placed himself in a relationship of both ally and competitor with his Nazi partner; he thought that Hitler would dedicate his forces to the northern, continental hemisphere, and thereby give Mussolini a free hand in southern Europe and the Mediterranean. The fascist general's directive to conduct a war "parallel" to that of Germany, with pre-established distinct and independent spheres of influence, was derived from this presumption. What Mussolini overlooked was the lack of an effective and loyal coordination between the two fas-

On June 10, 1940, the crowd that came together in Piazza Venezia in Rome applauded Mussolini's speech, in which (at left) he announced the declaration of war on France and Great Britain. In the months that preceded the entry into war, the regime's propaganda placed no limits on Italian claims, in particular toward France, mixing memories of the Risorgimento and colonial ambitions: Nice and the Savoy, Corsica, Tunis....

Italian soldiers in Libya (above), and in the mountains of Epirus in the winter of 1940. Involved on different fronts, and with too great a distance separating them, Italian troops were placed on the defensive very early. The attack against Greece, in particular, was a disaster.
Right, an 88-mm German anti-aircraft gun employed by Italian units in north Africa, 1941.

cist powers, the hidden jealousies between the two dictators, and the different rhythms of preparation and military potentials. After the defeat of France, Hitler launched operation "Sea Lion" against England, and *Il Duce* looked forward to the possibility of contributing to the razing of London, as Nazi planes had done to the city of Coventry. But Mussolini had to concern himself with the threat posed by the strong English navy, as well as other bulwarks of the British Empire in the Mediterranean (above all Malta) and in Africa — fronts that were extremely vast and distant from Italy; and which required great effort from a strategic viewpoint.

The "brigand" logic (as it was conceived by the fascist bosses themselves) of the parallel war led to the notion of attacking Greece. The assault was planned by Mussolini and Ciano for October 28, 1940, the anniversary of the march on Rome — a date that was to have augured well for the fate of the expedition. (This fetish for historical dates was comparable to the astrological obsessions of the Nazi bosses.)

The plan to bring about the ruin — literally to "smash the kidneys" — of Greece was a total failure: the Italian troops were thrown back and the little Greek army presented a serious threat to the Italian-held Albanian border. In the ice and mud of Balkan trenches, Italian soldiers began to pay the enormous price of the tragic fascist war.

On November 12, 1940, the British Navy subjected the military port of Taranto to an extremely fierce bombardment that put some of the best units of the Italian fleet out of service. On the Libyan front, things were no better: troops commanded by Graziani were limited to a difficult defense throughout December 1940 and January 1941, until General Wavell routed the Italians, taking 133,000 prisoners. In May 1941, the English reconquered Ethiopia, and Haile Selassie re-entered Addis Ababa. The Italian East African empire, to which fascism had devoted so many of its resources, and which had represented the first serious stage of the international crisis of the second half of the 1930s, was the first to fall.

Italian military fortunes were, by now, compromised, and in every case tied firmly to German initiatives. Only the intervention of Nazi troops in Yugoslavia and Greece permitted the Italians to get out of the Albanian quagmire discreetly. Yugoslavia was partitioned, and the Italian army transformed into an occupying force: the provinces of Cattaro, Lubiana and Spalato were annexed directly to Italy, and the crown of the puppet kingdom of Croatia given to the House of Savoy. But much more demanding was Mussolini's decision to stand at Hitler's side in the invasion of the Soviet Union on June 22, 1941. The Italian expeditionary force was progressively reinforced — in number, if not arms — until it constituted a true army of 230,000 men, the

Mussolini's desire to conduct a war in parallel with that of the Nazi ally soon showed itself to be a dangerous illusion. Only German intervention saved the Italian army from total disaster in Greece and Albania.

ARMIR, which would suffer severe decimation over the course of 1943.

Further, on September 30, 1940, Italy, Germany and Japan joined together in the Tripartite Pact, an alliance that, in the wake of the Japanese attack on December 7, 1941 on Pearl Harbor, dragged the two European nations into war with the United States. Italy's adversaries were multiplying at precisely the time the fortunes of war were taking a turn for the worst.

A Nation Suffers

If fascism was the minor partner in the Italian-German alliance, it had, nevertheless, contributed much to the enormous expansion of the fronts and theaters of war that, by now, spared almost no part of the world. As long as the war was fought far from Italian national borders, and as long as material and human losses remained limited, the home front did not concern fascist authorities. As the war progressed, however, the social situation could change, as could the Italian people's passive acquiescence to the regime's impositions.

In Verona, the Pasubio *division, departing for the Eastern front, marches before Mussolini. Begun in 1941, the Russian adventure concluded in 1943. During the disastrous retreat from the Don front alone over 70,000 Italians fell.*

For a time, the person of *Il Duce* had been compromised by rumors, but was less damaged by open criticism or invective than other leaders (the wealthy and privileged Ciano above all, but also the discredited successors to Starace in the secretariat of the PNF, such as Ettore Muti, Adelchi Serena, and Aldo Vidussoni — the regime's young and ambitious ministers and career men), who lived in a climate of corruption that could no longer be hidden from the eyes of the masses that were forced to support the brunt of the war. Eventually, the image of Mussolini himself tended to become clouded.

The leader was always distant now, no longer making the rounds through cities and localities that were festively decorated, and that once welcomed him with crowds; he no longer gave the impression that he shared the sacrifices of war with his people.

As Italo Calvino observed, the iconography of *Il Duce* had changed. After 1922, he began to dramatically transform his features: the physical defect of baldness was concealed by the complete shaving of his head; his

As long as the war was fought far from national borders, and as long as material and human losses remained limited, the domestic front did not concern fascist authorities. But as military losses became more apparent, the situation within the country began to change, as well.

prominent and threatening eyes were no longer portrayed directly, but in profile, exalting the famous strong-willed jaw. He had made himself harder, his eyes reduced to slits, while the helmet that covered his head completely transformed the *pater familias* into a lifeless statue, a deaf and mute commander.

With the mourning of soldiers' families, the ancient specters of poverty and famine also returned to circulation. The self-sufficiency program had already consumed the minimal resources and savings that had been accumulated by families. The rationing system gave rise to instances of market cornering for various items, and encouraged the growth of the black market. Rationing led to a reduced access to food (the daily ration of bread was lowered from 200 to 150 grams per person in 1942), accentuating the indigence especially of the urban working classes. Every reasonable person understood, by now, that the regime had exceeded the limits of credibility, making ridiculous provisions like the cultivation of "war gardens" — the churchyard of the Cathedral of Milan, covered with a planting of grain, certainly could not feed the people of the city.

Probably the clearest symptom of the progressive psychological distancing of the Italians from the regime was the growing practice of listening to enemy radio transmissions such as the celebrated Italian-language transmissions by Colonel Stevens of Radio London, which were held to be more objective and credible than official fascist information. Furthermore, in Italy, the Vatican Radio and the *Osservatore Romano* were followed carefully, while news emanating from every organ of the regime had lost almost all credibility in the eyes of the masses.

Mussolini in a portrait from the early years of the war. With the passage of time, the image of Il Duce *that was promulgated by fascist propaganda became progressively harder, accentuating characteristics such as the strong-willed jaw, or the martial aspect.*

This distancing from fascism and the move to an antifascist mentality began to be measured in terms of millions of people, no longer in terms of a few thousand opponents. The phenomenon, defined as "war-time antifascism" because of its moral nature rather than its political awareness, brought together clearly the link between fascism and war. The jokes and bitter stories against Mussolini began to assume the form of demonstrations of popular anger that demanded the end of the war, the end of fascism, bread, and peace.

During the Second World War, there was little sign of the draft-dodging and desertion that had been prominent during the First World War. But between 1942 and 1943, a growing tendency to (illegally) avoid the draft weakened the mobilization order imposed by the dictatorship, and undermined the integrity of the fascist

regime's base. And since all soldiers in the army were obligatorily registered in the party, the forced nature of the membership removed every last shred of truth from the "voluntary" nature of the members, as well as much of the credibility derived from the figures on paper.

Moreover, none of the fascist organizations understood how to assist the civil population with at least their presence or attention, and all were gradually supplanted by the Church. The personal prestige of the new Pope, Pius XII, grew at the expense of Mussolini and members of the government, who could rarely find a word of comfort for the suffering masses.

The line in Milan for food rationing cards in 1943, a year that witnessed a progressive sense of psychological alienation for Italians, as they became aware of the disastrous news coming from various fronts, even as they lived with the restrictions imposed by the wartime economy.

A group of Italian troops (bersaglieri) in Tunisia. The last Axis troops in northern Africa surrendered to the Allies on May 13, 1943.

The Fall of Mussolini and the Armistice

In the meantime, while Rommel plugged the breaches in the Italian front in north Africa, the arrival of the Allies in Morocco made it clear that the Mediterranean would become the next principal theater of the war, and that the Italian mainland, which had already suffered terrible bombardments during the fall of 1942, in Genoa and other northern cities, would receive the brunt of the attack. After the defeat at El Alamein, the Italian-German forces in Libya capitulated in May 1943, with 200,000 Italian prisoners falling into enemy hands. In June, the Allied force occupied Pantelleria and, at the beginning of July, landed in Sicily, thereby initiating the invasion of Italy, which had been characterized by Churchill as the soft underbelly of the Axis.

A last changing of the guard imposed on his ministers by Mussolini in February 1943, which replaced the principal leaders and collaborators with second-rank figures, failed to revitalize the population's morale.

The fascist bosses were stunned to learn the previously classified news that major strikes had broken out in several industrial cities in March 1943. Workers stood with their arms crossed in order to win salary increases and economic benefits, but here and there, protests against the war were also heard. To the modern observer, this episode may seem minor, if not insignifi-

cant. But Hitler's incredulity in the face of such actions, and his furious responses, explain the importance that strikes held in a fascist country — especially one that was involved in total war. The German dictator was indignant over this show of antifascism, and it is possible that, from this point, Hitler began to nourish certain doubts about Mussolini's capacity to keep the situation under control. The regime, in fact, kept the strikes of March 1943, under control by means of both repression and economic concessions to the workers. This was the first strike in Nazi/Fascist-controlled Europe since the 1941 strike in Amsterdam, held to protest the deportation of Jews.

The communists were among the most active organizers of strikes, but the other antifascist parties were also secretly reconstituting themselves. Some, like the Christian Democrats under De Gasperi and Giuseppe Dossetti (heirs of the *Partito Popolare*, the People's Party) took new names. Others, such as Ferruccio Parri's Action Party, arose bearing ties to the former party of Justice and Liberty. Re-establishing contacts, exchanging propaganda, creating a network of solidarity that contributed to the demise of the former obstacles of diffidence and mutual suspicion, the antifascist parties were preparing to resume their role as an active and effective presence in the life of Italian society.

Americans enter Monreale, the small Sicilian city lying just outside Palermo. Operation "Husky," the invasion of Sicily, began on July 10, 1943, and involved Patton's Seventh Army and the Eighth English Armored Division under Montgomery. Italian and German troops abandoned the island on August 18, 1943, after Mussolini had already fallen.

It is, nevertheless, a fact that these factions did not yet have the strength to overthrow fascism with an insurrection. The regime was overturned, essentially, because of the outcome of the war: Sicily was lost and the invasion of the peninsula seemed at hand and inevitable. By the summer of 1943, a double conspiracy that originated within the establishment — having components among the fascist leadership on one hand and royalty on the other — had taken root. This plot anticipated an openly antifascist action from the population itself. It has been said, not without reason, that the forces of the papacy had deluded themselves into believing that it would be possible to give birth to a fascism without Mussolini, to an authoritarian regime capable of rescuing what was salvageable by sacrificing *Il Duce*.

On the night of July 24, 1943, although it had not been convened for years, the Grand Council held its last meeting. A proposal by Grandi to restore the conduct of the war to the king was accepted, and Mussolini

THE JULY 25ᵀᴴ ANNOUNCEMENT

The Grand Council of Fascism, in an order of the day, voted to withdraw its confidence in Mussolini on the night of July 24, 1943. The 10:45 P.M. radio broadcast on July 25 gave notice that: "His Majesty the King and Emperor has accepted the resignation of Cavalier Benito Mussolini from the charges of Head of the Government, Prime Minister, and Secretary of State, and has nominated Cavalier and Marshal of Italy, Pietro Badoglio, to the position of Head of the Government, Prime Minister and Secretary if State." No news of Mussolini's fate was provided.

Two proclamations were then transmitted. In the first, the king announced that he would assume command of all armed forces and warned that "no deviation will be tolerated, no recrimination will be permitted"; he affirmed that Italy would find the way to recovery "in respect of the institutions that had

always been its comfort in times of ascendancy."

In the second, Badoglio affirmed that, "By order of His Majesty the King and Emperor, I assume the military governance of the country with full powers. The war continues. Italy, hit hard in its invaded provinces, in its destroyed cities, keeps its word, as proud custodian of its thousand-year tradition.

"Let us close the ranks around His Majesty, the King and Emperor, living image of the fatherland and example to all. The charge I have received is clear and precise. It will be scrupulously executed, and whoever deludes himself into thinking that he will be able to hamper the normal course of events, or attempt to upset public order, will inevitably be punished." ∎

was reduced in rank by the leadership. This session is viewed by many historians as an event of fundamental historic importance. In reality, it did nothing more than give Victor Emmanuel III the pretext to summon Mussolini and remove his trust in the fascist leader. The aged sovereign, together with other diplomats and military aides, had prepared the coup d'etat with care. Mussolini was arrested and replaced by Badoglio. The radio announced the dismissal (not the arrest) of the former *Duce* on the evening of July 25, giving rise to many demonstrations of relief, and even joy among the population.

Almost incredibly, the fascists seemed unresponsive: not one of the "musketeers of *Il Duce*" raised a finger in protest; the heads of the party and the militia consigned their organizations to the military leadership. The black shirts, the fez, the fascist uniforms all disappeared; and not one fascist remembered, the following day, having worn in his buttonhole the *cimice* (as the insignia of the PNF was sometimes called). There was a complete and total disappearance of the fascist leaders and of followers who could have shed light on the limits of the consensus that had formed around the dic-

Several days after the fall of fascism, the army presides over fascist headquarters in Milan, while signs of the regime are removed. Badoglio's radio message, announcing the resignation of Mussolini, was greeted with shows of jubilation almost everywhere, in the belief that the war would be ended in a short time.
To the left, Marshal Pietro Badoglio (1871–1956).

On September 9, 1943, the flight of the king and Badaglio from Rome was the coup de grace *inflicted on the state and nation.*

tatorship — potentially a great loss to historians.

Immediately after the fall of Mussolini, the king and Badoglio communicated to the country that they would tolerate no trials of officials of the former regime, nor breaches of public order, and that the war would continue, with Italy fighting at the side of the German ally. The overthrow was void of any content that was openly antifascist or democratic.

The government, composed primarily of technicians and soldiers, got along for several weeks trying, on one hand, to block the legalization of antifascist parties, and on the other, to establish secret talks with the Allies that might result in a possible exit from the conflict for Italy.

During the "forty-five days," as the period between July 25 and September 8, 1943, came to be known, the police and army opened fire on several occasions

A *mob dismantles the symbols of fascism in the streets of Rome. In the weeks that followed July 25, the Badoglio government proscribed the legalization of antifascist parties, and never sought the support of the population in its improvised effort to break with the Germans.*

against unarmed demonstrators seeking peace, liberation from forced labor, or from constraints imposed by the Special Tribunal, or relief from fascist persecution. Labor unions and political parties continued to act under semi-clandestine conditions, while Victor Emmanuel III and Badoglio refused to appeal directly to the people or consider them allies in the attempt to break free of the German yoke. In the meantime, the German army had dispatched eight divisions into Italy — a number nearly equaling the number of effective Italian troops.

Efforts by Badoglio's emissaries to negotiate with the Allies failed to obtain anything less than a request for unconditional surrender from General Eisenhower, the commander in chief of the Allied forces. The Italian armistice with the Allies, signed on September 5 at Cassibile in Sicily, was announced only three days later, while Victor Emmanuel III, the royal family and Badoglio himself, with other generals, were departing from Rome in the direction of the Abruzzi coast, and from there by sea to Brindisi — an area beyond German reach.

The flight to Pescara in Abruzzi, and the shameful abandonment of the capital, were the coup de grace inflicted on the nation and state by several of its highest officeholders. Victor Emmanuel III and Badoglio had succeeded in being recognized by the Allies as the sole legitimate forces representing Italy; now, they were also the guarantors of the military defeat. But it was a group of several civilians that improvised the spontaneous defense of Rome against German attack and gave life to one of the first episodes of the Resistance. During that same period, on September 9, an antifascist party group coalesced in the form of the Committee of National Liberation, which called on the people "to struggle and fight for the re-conquest of Italy's place among the assembly of free nations."

A *cannon used on September 9, 1943, during the defense of Port San Paolo in Rome. During the convulsive hours that followed the king's flight to Pescara and the announcement of the Italian armistice with the allies, soldiers and civilians sought spontaneously to oppose the entry of German troops into the capital, giving birth to the first episode of the Resistance.*

Chapter 8

A DIFFICULT
LEGACY

THE FALL OF MUSSOLINI DID NOT MARK THE END OF FASCISM. AFTER THE REPUBLIC OF SALÒ, THAT BLOODY EPILOGUE OF THE FASCIST ERA, AND AFTER THE STRUGGLE FOR LIBERATION... EVEN AFTER THE DEATH OF ITS FOUNDER, FASCISM'S STORY CONTINUED TO UNFURL IN REPUBLICAN ITALY, UNDER OTHER GUISES AND DIFFERENT NAMES.

Chronologically speaking, the history of fascism and the history of Italy between 1922 and 1943 were superimposed on one another and intersected, but without entirely coinciding. During that period not everything Italian women and men produced, both economically and culturally, bespoke the dominating power of fascism. But the dictatorship, thanks to its propaganda apparatus, was able to appropriate and vaunt as its own most of the concrete results produced by society such as technological and scientific progress, new areas of human knowledge, and successes in the improvement of hygiene, health and education.

In 1943, the connection between the history of fascism and that of Italy was brought to an end. From that point on, the two proceeded in very different and relatively independent ways. Formal fascism may have drawn to a close between 1943 and 1945, but its story continued through succeeding decades up to the present day. Though no longer in a position of power, its threatening, and insidious presence has not disappeared.

With September 8 and the monarchy's betrayal, the state suffered the most serious crisis since unification. Italy found itself divided in two, occupied in the center and north by invading Germans, and in the south by the British and Americans. All bureaucratic and administrative struc-

The Gallery and the main hospital in Milan, bombed by the allies in 1943. After September 8, Italy found itself split in two: occupied by the Allies in the south and by the Germans in the center and north. In this already serious military situation, fascism made its last stand, and the puppet state of Salò was created.

tures underwent total collapse: the economy was, in essence, reduced to the black market, and the armed forces disintegrated, permitting the Germans to imprison 600,000 Italian soldiers in Germany. The fighting would touch every corner of the national territory, little by little, as the front retreated toward the north. The entire civil population would be affected by the defeat, with no way of escape, no exceptions.

The Italian Social Republic

By September 8 the German secret services had identified where Mussolini was being held under arrest by Badoglio's *carabinieri*, and succeeded in liberating the former leader and transferring him to Germany. Under Nazi protection via Radio Munich, Mussolini was able to appeal to the Italian people, announcing the constitution of a new

state, the *Repubblica Sociale Italiana* (Italian Social Republic), or RSI. This was not a truly sovereign state, because its jurisdiction coincided with the regions under German military administration. These areas of northeastern Italy had in fact been annexed to the Reich.

The republican institutional form had been chosen by Mussolini as a defense against the humiliation suffered by Victor Emmanuel III, but the new state did not at all correspond to a true republic: in essence the RSI was a puppet state, a regime in close collaboration with Germany. Nor should the name lead one to believe that a program of "socialization" was under way; this was never the case. Instead, the RSI behaved in the demagogic manner that was typical of fascism. It attempted to recast itself with a simplicity that recalled the jargon of the fascist state in its infancy, replete with anti-capitalist phraseology. What remained of the state apparatus, with its prefectures and *questure* (state police headquarters) was utilized by the Mussolini regime to assist the Nazis in their exploitation of material and human resources in areas under their control. In this sense, Republican neo-fascism had some success, showing its more truculent and brutal face as it repressed resistance movements and terrorized the civil population.

The new fascist party retained only a small minority of PNF members; the militia, though, was reconstituted under the name of the Republican National Guard, and integrated as a unit of the *carabinieri*, while the fascist police were very active with their network of informers. But the Social Republic never really succeeded in reconstituting an army of its own under Marshal Graziani. Mussolini's ambitions of being able to play a role in determining the outcome of the world conflict, or even the conflict under way in Italy, were destined to vanish. The RSI was never in a position to establish stable diplomatic relations as a true sovereign state; nor did it have a capital city, with its vari-

A formation of women auxiliaries of the Italian Social Republic in Milan, September 1943. Notwithstanding the fact that Mussolini's call to arms for the "honor" of Italy obtained a certain degree of success, especially among the young, the armed forces of the new state, entrusted to Marshal Graziani, never became a true army, and were employed mainly as a police force.

The name of the Italian Social Republic was officially adopted by the new fascist state on November 25, 1943: until then, as an indication of the true precariousness of that title, the Republican State of Italy and the Republican National State were used at various times. This was a one-party police state, based on precepts derived from a vague, demagogical ideology. Nevertheless, an 18-point program was prepared at the Republican Fascist party congress held in Verona in November 1943. This manifesto of the republic of Salò provided for the election of the head of state every five years; declared the fall of the monarchy; convoked a constituent assembly; declared that the Party was the sole agent responsible for the education of the people.

Although it granted that registration was not obligatory for public employment; it established that the religion of the Republic was Catholicism, that Jews were foreigners, and that in the current war they were to be seen as belonging to the enemy nation. It invoked the need for "vital spaces," and advocated the fashioning of a "European community," as well as the liquidation of "centuries-old British plots against the continent." It also affirmed certain principles of a socialist nature:

9. The foundation of the Social Republic, and its primary objective, is work — manual, technical, and intellectual — in every form.

10. Private property, the fruit of work and individual savings and representative of an integrated human personality, is guaranteed by the state. The state, however, must not attempt to disintegrate the physical and moral personalities of men through the exploitation of their work.

11. In the national economy, all things that, by dimension and function exceed the interests of the individual, thereby enter into the interests of the collective and belong to the sphere of activity of the state.

12. In every business (individually, privately, part or wholly state-owned), representatives of technicians and workers will cooperate intimately with, and be kept in awareness of, the concern's financial well-being, and will share equally in the profits within the reserve fund, which is the fruit of capital stock. In some establishments, this may come about as an extension of the prerogatives of the current commissions of the factory." ■

ous leaders being dispersed among the provincial capitals of Lombardy and the Veneto.

The regime was also known as the Republic of Salò, after the small town on the banks of Lake Garda where, in the Villa Feltrinelli, Mussolini had established residence. Mussolini had surrounded himself with Nazi sympathizers and second-rank collaborators who were faithful to him, such as Pavolini, Ricci, Farinacci, and Buffarini Guidi; more celebrated fascist adherents to the new republic were very limited in number, and in the area of culture, reduced almost exclusively to Giovanni Gentile and Filippo Tommaso Marinetti.

The ferocity of neo-fascism and the climate of the blood-feud that had been set in motion were immediately revealed at the beginning of 1944, in the Verona trials against the ex-leaders who had voted against *Il Duce* at the Grand Council on July 25, 1943. In addition to the "quadrumvir" De Bono, those condemned to death even included Mussolini's son-in-law, Galeazzo Ciano.

Resistance and Liberation

Violence and the most extreme forms of fanaticism, particularly anti-Semitism, and the almost total acceptance of Nazi ideology were the essential traits of Republican neo-fascism. The uniforms themselves, with emblems derived from skulls, the hymn-like songs performed at a time of death, tragically exemplified a nihilistic madness that brought together authentic criminals, intolerant despots, and disillusioned and naïve youth.

No episode is more revealing of Mussolini's distance from reality, of his inability to comprehend the political situation that was mounting against him, than the following: he asked his military chiefs to obtain copies of royal decrees dating from 1863 against southern brigands, to extract some sort of inspiration or legal justification for the

One of the last images of Galeazzo Ciano, imprisoned in Verona. With the trial in Verona, which concluded in a series of death sentences, including the executions by firing squad of Ciano and De Bono, Mussolini obtained revenge against members of the Grand Council who, on July 25, 1943, had signed the order introduced by Grandi.
Left, the Villa of the Ursulines at Salò on Lake Garda, site of the headquarters of the Social Republic.

The partisans enter Milan after the liberation of the city on April 25, 1945. Heading the parade, in the center, are Ferruccio Parri, Raffaele Cadorna, and Luigi Longo. The order to begin the general insurrection in the large cities of the north was given by the National Liberation Committee in the spring of 1945: Milan, Turin, and Genoa were liberated before the arrival of the Allies.

fight against antifascist forces — in neo-fascist jargon the "rebels" and "bandits." But the Resistance and the National Liberation Committee (CLN) were now in a position to conduct political and military activities that went beyond mere acts of sabotage. They were laying the foundation for a national insurrection to free the country of Nazi/Fascists and to clear the way for a democratic reformation of the nation.

After the liberation of Rome in June 1944, the antifascist parties gave birth to the Bonomi government; Florence and Tuscany were liberated in August and local powers were assumed by the CLN. In the north, an increasingly organized partisan army under the leadership of Parri, head of the Action Party, and the Communist Longo seriously engaged a number of German military units.

The neo-fascists were given an opportunity to distinguish themselves alongside the ss units of Kappler and Reder, in particular in their reprisals against the civilian population (including the slaughtering of the elderly, and of women and children), and their capturing of partisans and Jews, who would be destined for Nazi extermination camps. In addition, increasing numbers of Italians were

consigned to German military production sectors; they were either employed in the north or sent directly to Germany to perform forced labor.

The Social Republic tended, with the passing months, to disappear from the ranks of effective protagonists in the war. When the British and Americans were in a position to unleash the final offensive against the Germans in spring of 1945, the CLN gave the order to begin the insurrection, and the great northern cities were quickly liberated by the partisans. Mussolini attempted in vain to avoid capture, disguising himself by wearing the uniform of a German soldier. But he was captured, in company with his mistress, Clara Petacci, and executed by order of the CLN. By the end of April, all of Italy had been liberated.

Two of the protagonists behind Mussolini's capture at Dongo: Count Pier Luigi Bellini delle Stelle (Pedro), commander of the partisan brigade that intercepted Mussolini's vehicle, and Urbano Lazzari (Bill), who arrested Il Duce and his companion, Clara Petacci.

The Missed Opportunity

Fascism was silenced, but the new Italian government had no wish to proceed with a general, intensive purge of fascists. Instead, certain legal decrees authorized trials of fascist bosses, of prominent figures of the regime who were responsible for having brought Italy to war and defeat, of active fascist party and militia members who

THE END OF MUSSOLINI

On the last leg of his journey, Mussolini hoped to be able to find cover in neutral Switzerland, and fled from Milan disguised in a German uniform and helmet, on a truck carrying German soldiers in retreat. He was stopped and discovered by a group of partisans who, by order of the CLN, arrested Il Duce on April 27 and executed him by firing squad on the following day, at Giulino di Mezzegra, in the vicinity of Dongo. The execution was a symbolic act that differentiated the fate of Il Duce, tried by representatives of the Italian people, from that of the Nazi bosses, who were tried by an international tribunal of the victorious Allied Powers at Nuremberg. The bodies of Mussolini, of his mistress Clara Petacci, and the other fascist leaders who were executed near Dongo were displayed in Piazza Loreto in Milan (the same piazza in which the bodies of fifteen hostages, executed by the fascists after German instigation, were displayed in August 1944). They were shown to the crowds in Milan hanging by their feet, heads hanging down — a crude and terrible image, which writer Italo Calvino would not have wished on anyone, except all dictators currently living in the world. ∎

*P*ietro Nenni (on the left), Palmiro Togliatti and Alcide De Gasperi (first and second, respectively, from the right) at the time of the formation of the government that succeeded Parri's (December 10, 1945). The new government quickly imposed a moderate pace on the purge, and Communist Party secretary Togliatti, in his capacity as justice minister, conceded a broad amnesty in June 1946.

had committed political crimes, and of those who had collaborated with the Germans after September 8, 1943. In this way the state administration managed a substantial purge of the fascists.

After the first, brief term of the Parri government, De Gasperi took over near the end of 1945. Though he was the head of a coalition government that included all of the parties of the CLN, the Christian Democratic leader imposed a pace that was clearly more moderate than that of his predecessor. His government set out a program that in various ways attempted substantial institutional renewal and economic reconstruction.

But De Gasperi felt that the antifascist values of CLN members who had given life to the struggle against the Social Republic were only transitory. His justice minister, Togliatti, proclaimed a general amnesty in June 1946, that generously spared the overwhelming majority of fascists. Nenni tried to establish firm criteria in ascertaining what were the profits of the regime, and in purging those who had made a successful career with the fascists, but the operation was limited to a very small number of cases, and finally abandoned under the new political situation that had arisen by May 1947, which witnessed the

exclusion of the left from the national government.

Of the 800,000 employees and state dependants, only 1,874 were dismissed and 671 forced to resign. But even the majority of these were somehow reintegrated into their former positions. The personal fortunes of 500 profiteers were estimated at the time to be 20 billion lire, but the law authorizing confiscation was never enforced. The purge, therefore, was quickly dispensed with.

In the meantime, Italians, including women who for the first time were exercising their right to vote in the June 2, 1946 referendum, had selected the republic as the preferred institutional form of the new post-Fascist state. The defeat of the monarchy meant, in the medium and long-term, the elimination of an institutional center of power that had always seemed a point of reference in any shift toward the right of the political spectrum.

In 1947, Italy signed a peace treaty with its former enemies, asked to be admitted to the UN, and in 1949, joined the Atlantic Alliance. From January 1, 1948, the new constitution took effect. With this internal change and the shift of the national political axis toward the center, a change dictated by the opening phase of the international Cold War, the transition from Fascist to Republican Italy was

The announcement of the results of the Institutional Referendum of June 2, 1946. On that occasion, which witnessed the affirmation of the Republican form of government, Italian women exercised the right to vote for the first time. With the victory of the Republic, King Umberto II (who assumed the throne after the abdication of his father, Victor Emmanuel III in May, 1946) left Italy on June 13, 1946.

The Coltano prison camp, near Pisa, where prisoners of the Social Republic were kept after the end of the war. Below, Marshal Graziani takes part in a meeting of the Movimento Sociale (MSI) sympathizers in 1952. The purge following the end of fascism was superficial: Graziani himself was freed and able to enroll in the msi as early as 1950.

rendered less radical. Aside from Mussolini and the few leaders who were tried in April 1945, most fascist leaders survived with little difficulty, taking refuge for a time in the Vatican, or, as in the case of Bottai, in the foreign legion. (Bottai later returned to Italy as a journalist and newspaper director.) Others took exile in countries supported by fascist regimes; this was the case for Grandi, who moved to Portugal, but numerous others found refuge in Franco's Spain, or with sympathetic dictatorships in South America. Some ex-secretaries of the pnf, former ministers and members of the Grand Council continued to live and work in Italy, at times holding positions and exercising responsibilities that were well compensated.

Many of the 1,204 Italian war prisoners appearing on certain UN commission lists remained unpunished. Only a few military officers were tried, and of those who were, almost all, including Graziani (who had assumed command of the armed forces of Salò) and Mario Roatta (former commander of the secret services), were given light sentences, At the top of the UN's list of Ethiopian war criminals was Badoglio, who was a free citizen living in Italy, and prominent in the list presented by Yugoslavia, were Taddeo Orlando and Achille Marazzo who, in 1947, were in service to the regime in the capacities of secretary general of the defense ministry and undersecretary of the interior ministry.

At the foreign ministry, the tip of the fascist diplomatic iceberg, there were obvious changes, especially among the ranks of the ambassadors, with the nominations of antifascists Giuseppe Saragat and Alberto Tarchiani to the posts in Paris and Washington, respectively. On the other hand, among the first Italian representatives to the UN was one diplomat who had announced fascist Italy's departure from the League of Nations in 1937. Prefects, some of whom had been in service to the RSI, were seen as eligible for reassignment, rather than as candidates for expulsion; magistrates of the Special Tribunal retained their right to a pension; and several signers of the racial manifesto of 1938, such as Sabato Visco, who was then president of the Faculty of Sciences at the University of Rome, retained prestigious university positions even after 1945.

The Legacy and Shadow of Fascism

The crime of defending or exalting fascism was recognized in normal law — and understood to be one of the legacies of the *Ventennio* — but was among the most tolerated to emerge from post-fascist Italy, even in cases where there was no lack of proof or evidence. Equally problem-

THE REPUBLICAN CONSTITUTION

If the regime collapsed in 1943 and Mussolini's political parabola ended with the liberation of Italy on April 25, 1945, the end of fascism in a historic sense, may be identified with a more complex process, that witnessed the advent of the Republic on June 2, 1946, and the initiation of the Constitution on January 1, 1948. This document expresses better than any other the historical achievement of the fascist experiment, particularly in its first articles, dedicated to fundamental principles:

"**Art.1.** Italy is a democratic republic, founded on work. Sovereignty belongs to the people, who exercise it within the form and limits of the Constitution.

Art. 2. The Republic recognizes and guarantees the inviolable rights of man, both as an individual and in social formations, in which he expresses his personality, and asks to fulfill his political, economic and social responsibilities [...]

Art. 3. All citizens have equal social dignity, and are equal before the law, regardless of sex, race, language, religion, political opinion, personal or social condition [...].

Art. 5. The Republic, one and indivisible, recognizes and promotes local autonomy; it practices broad administrative decentralization in services that depend on the state; it adjusts the principles and methods of its legislation to the needs of autonomy and decentralization [...].

Art. 10. The Italian Judicial structure conforms to the generally recognized norms of international law. The legal status of a foreigner is regulated by the law, in conformity with international norms and treaties. The foreigner to whom the effective exercise of freedom [...] as guaranteed by the Constitution in Italy is blocked in his own country has the right to exile in the territory of the Republic, in accordance with conditions established by law. The extradition of a foreigner for political crimes is not permitted.

Art. 11. Italy repudiates war, both as an instrument that offends the liberty of other peoples and as a means of resolving international controversies; it consents, in conditions of equality with other states, to the limitations of sovereignty that may be required to maintain a degree of order that guarantees peace and justice among nations; it promotes and favors international organizations that are devoted to this end." ∎

Giorgio Almirante (center), together with members of the Movimento Sociale. The party, which Almirante continued to serve as secretary until his death, was founded in Rome on December 26, 1946, amid the remnants of the Social Republic (the Party's name clearly and explicitly recalling that of the preceding Republic). Its creation circumvented the law that was to have blocked reconstitution of the fascist party.

atic was the prohibition of "reorganization, under any form, of the dissolved fascist party," provided for by the twelfth and final interim "Dispositions" of the constitution. This provision was, in essence, circumvented by the creation, as early as 1946, of a party that was clearly of fascist inspiration, but named by its founders the *Movimento Sociale Italiano* (MSI).

In the late 1940s and early 1950s, this organization met with less success than the monarchist parties or the right-wing movement known as *l'Uomo qualunque* (The Everyman), which challenged Christian Democratic control in several southern Italian electoral districts. Subsequently, however, the MSI also succeeded in affirming an electoral presence, one that has asserted itself reasonably well, gathering between five and six percent of the national political electorate, and often in excess of ten percent in large cities, such as Rome and Naples.

The MSI succeeded in guiding the radical right-wing opposition to a constitutional and democratic arrangement; it played some role in supporting the government led by the Christian Democrat Fernando Tambroni, whose intentions of moving national politics to the right were defeated in 1960, thanks only to energetic popular

protests. The MSI also maintains that it contributed, with its votes, to the election of at least two presidents of the Republic; but it also, in various ways, covered actions that were openly subversive, like the attempted coup of Junio Valerio Borghese in 1970. The party also secretly sustained several groups that had distanced themselves from the MSI, such as Terza Posizione (Third Position), Ordine Nuovo (The New Order), and Ordine Nero (The Black Order) — from

which right-wing terrorism sprang. The political matrix behind the numerous killings that bloodied Italy from 1964 to 1984, and resulted in the deaths of hundreds of innocent victims, was legitimately defined as fascist; their situation stood in clear contrast to the democratic consolidation that was under way during these decades. Moreover, external signs of a fascist pseudo-cultural and behavioral continuity became manifest in the form of skirmishes between opposing soccer fans, the use of the Roman salute (with the arm stiffly extended forward), insults against Jews, graffiti singing the praises of the SS and signs of the swastika.

Riots in Reggio Emilia, 1960, during the protest against the Tambroni government. The government had been formed in March of that year, and maintained its position in parliament with the determining support of MSI votes.

The passing years — and increased distance from direct affiliation with "historic" Fascism — have, in any case, noticeably changed the intensity and degree of institutional danger posed by these fascist challenges, which have maintained themselves through connivance and secrecy, within certain sectors of the state apparatus (for instance "deviant" secret societies such as the Masonic lodges, typified by P2, or auxiliary criminal organizations such as the Mafia and Camorra.)

The disappearance of the monarchy, and the non-presidential nature of the Italian Republic, have minimized the possibility that an authoritative endorsement might eventually be given to a candidate sympathetic to the designs of a subversive right, or that a fascist terrorism might obtain results. Further, the decline of nationalism and of imperialistic dreams, the failures of the fascist states in the Iberian peninsula, Greece and Latin America, and the resultant shortcoming of any international dimension of the fascist phenomenon, make it a likely proposition that what Mussolini exalted in 1932 as "the fascist century" is about to come to an end. While of limited reliability, a 1980s poll indicated that 90 percent of Italians believed fascism and terrorism to have been among the gravest dangers in the nation's history, even though 30 percent made an exception for Mussolini himself, whom they continued to see in a favorable light. This is yet another sign of the ambiguity of the fascist legacy.

From 1993 to 1995, the Italian political landscape changed completely. Gianfranco Fini, the successor to Almirante at the helm of the MSI, dissolved the party, and gave birth to a new entity, the *Alleanza Nazionale* (AN). Fini considers himself to be a "post-fascist," and while maintaining that the fascist epoch has been completely phased out, he esteems Mussolini as the greatest politician of this century. In a recent AN congress session, Fini embraced democratic values recognizing the positive significance of antifascism. The objectives of the new party are the construction of a modern "right"; a presidency, intended as a concentration of representative and executive powers; nationalism adapted to our times (the AN rejected the Maastricht treaty); and statism, or the maintenance of a strong state presence in the economy.

The disappearance of the Christian Democrats and dispersion of its directing group and electorate, have created a power vacuum favorable to a strong revival of the right. This has been facilitated by mechanisms of the new but inefficient "majority" system that was experimented with in 1994. At the March elections of that year, the AN won 13 percent of the vote, or twice that obtained by the MSI during the previous year, and was therefore able to participate, as an ally of *Forza Italia* and the *Lega Nord*, in the short-lived Berlusconi government. From that point on, the AN appears to have successfully occupied a stronger position within the center-right "Polo." The party seems in fact to have posed a leadership problem for the entire coalition, a situation that has spawned a poorly masked rivalry between Fini and Berlusconi.

The AN seems to appeal to (1) a portion of the salaried middle-class that is fearful of losing jobs and social status; (2) a diverse and angry group of anti-tax protesters; and (3) followers of the new xenophobic radicals (in particular, those objecting to the presence of new "extra-community" immigrants) and those that have organized hostile acts against gypsies.

During the brief legislature of 1994–96, AN parliamentarians unleashed tumults and riots that recalled, at a distance of 70 years, the scorn displayed by Mussolini and the first fascist deputies toward parliamentary democracy and their political adversaries. It is certainly not by chance that the most alarmist comments on the actual behavior and practices of the AN come from outside observers and

Fighting in the piazza in Genoa, June 1960. Feeling the strength afforded it by the Tambroni government, the MSI decided to hold its congress in Genoa. The city responded with a general mobilization. In the ensuing street fighting among police, fascists, and antifascists, several hundred were wounded. The Tambroni government resigned on July 19. Left, members of the Movimento Sociale *salute with arms outstretched from the balcony of a party headquarters.*

Giorgio Almirante at the editorial offices of Il secolo d'Italia *(The Italian Century), an organ of the Movimento Sociale Italiano. Right, inside the* Banca dell'Agricoltura *in Milan after the bomb explosion that, on December 12, 1969, caused 16 deaths and over 100 wounded. This attack was one of the many dark pages that appeared during the post-war period, in which the activities of the Italian "right" were clearly aimed at destabilizing the state.*

the international press, rather than Italian public opinion. The political right under the AN, in any case, has become a stable presence on the Italian political scene, while the MSI remains at its margins.

An Unfinished Balance Sheet

The history of half a century of the Italian republic was deeply scarred during its early years by the results of the formidable fascist experiment, which dampened much of the innovative impact of political, institutional and constitutional change that occurred during the period between 1945 and 1947.

The slogans and signs symbolizing fascism were quickly removed; but while these superficial changes were made, agencies and practices that originated during the *Ventennio* often remained in force, precisely because of the peculiar nature of government administration during that epoch. The breadth of the public sector of the economy, as well as of the state agencies that were created by fascism, had the effect of blocking the modernization of the social state. The hollow promises of free competition, and the development of a private entrepreneurial class that was free of a subordinate relationship with political power groups are still a long way from being realized.

The precise balance sheet of fascism's legacy remains to be constructed in the field of historical studies. The attempt has begun in recent times, though at a distance from the *Ventennio*, itself.

The continuity of the state in terms of men and of groups, if not institutions, has, for example, been noteworthy. The constitutional charter itself, so advanced and progressive, was forced to include in its article 7 the 1929 agreements between the fascist state and the Vatican. Yet the exasperating centralizing tendency of fascism was among the factors that contributed to the delay in introducing a regional framework. This came into effect only in 1970, over twenty years after the approval of the 1948 constitution, which had ignored it. Further, the Italian Republic had to operate, essentially, within the existing parameters of the school system, the magistrature, the police, and the bureaucracy that had been inherited from the past. This naturally had incalculable effects in terms of encouraging the persistence of certain habits, procedures, and administrative practices. Even today the administration can keep citizens at a distance, mimicking, in a way, the Kingdom of Italy's relations with its subjects.

With regard to the legal establishment, the fascist legacy was not one of hypothetical generalities or superficial modifications of a broad-based reform. Rather, it was quite specific, and included, with some amendments, the penal (1930) and civil (1941) codes, the banking law (1938), the law governing care and maintenance of Italy's artistic heritage (1939), as well as urban planning in general (1942), and finally, the state treasury's urban land register (1939).

The legacy of fascism in terms of mind-set and customs — which are traditionally slow to change — must still be adequately examined by the appropriate scholars; among other effects, fascism worked to worsen many characteristics that were viewed as "backward" even in pre-1922 Italian society.

Fascism's legacy in terms of mental attitude and customs — categories that are traditionally slow to change — continues to await adequate treatment by scholars. Nevertheless, fascism had the effect of worsening or crystallizing those aspects of Italian civil society perceived to be "backward," even before the advent of Mussolini. It is certain that these social conditions acted as a growth medium by which authoritarianism, deleterious conformism, and corruption grew to the status of a system. Moreover, many of these socio-political ills have continued

On the right, Gianfranco Fini, successor to Giorgio Almirante as head of the MSI, and today secretary of the Alleanza Nazionale (AN).

to threaten the nation during the period of the post-fascist democracy.

The Church, which both before and after the innovations introduced by Vatican II was the traditional and hierarchically organized support of the family, and of both minors and women, is one of the less visible sites over which the shadow of fascism extended.

The critical judgment by those who observe a lack of correspondence between the powerful economic development of the Italy that had just emerged from the abyss of fascism and a lost war on the one hand, and the growth, maturation, and widespread diffusion of the shared values taught in schools on the other, is found to be valid. Many Italians, it seems, demonstrate less attachment and devotion to civic values and the history taught in schools than to the energy they dedicate to work, leisure, and the consumption of goods. In a mass society that in many materialistic ways is vital and modern, the struggle to maintain steady cultural, moral, and civil progress promises to be lengthy, though it is worth being fought for many reasons; paramount among these are the fundamental principles that constitute the foundation of the Italian Republic.

Bibliography

■ Affron, Matthew and Mark Antliff, eds. *Fascist Visions: Art and Ideology in France and Italy*. Princeton University Press, 1997.

■ Bissel, Richard. *Fascist Italy and Nazi Germany: Comparison and Contrast*. Cambridge University Press, 1996.

■ Bosworth, R. J. B. *The Italian Dictatorship: Problems and Perspectives in the Interpretation of Mussolini and Fascism*. Edward Arnold, 1998.

■ Carsten, Francis. *The Rise of Fascism*. University of California Press, 1982.

■ DeGrazia, Victoria. *How Fascism Ruled Women: Italy, 1922–1945*. University of California Press, 1992.

■ Ferraresi, Franco. *Threats to Democracy: The Radical Right in Italy After the War*. Princeton University Press, 1996.

■ Gentile, Emilio. *The Sacralization of Politics in Fascist Italy*. Harvard University Press, 1996.

■ Holmes, Roger W. *Idealism of Giovanni Gentile*. AMS Press, 1978.

■ Lamb, Richard. *War in Italy 1943–1945: A Brutal Story*. Da Capo Press, 1996.

■ Lyttelton, Adrian. *Italian Fascism from Pareto to Gentile, 1919–1929*. 1974.

■ Mack-Smith, Denis. *Mussolini*. Random House, 1983.

■ Moravia, Alberto. *The Conformist*. Steerforth Press, 1999.

■ Moseley, Ray. *Mussolini's Shadow: The Double Life of Count Galeazzo Ciano*. Yale University Press, 2000.

■ Mussolini, Benito. *My Rise and Fall*. Da Capo Press, 1998.

■ Payne, Stanley G. *A History of Fascism, 1914–1945*. University of Wisconsin Press, 1995.

■ Pollard, John F. *The Fascist Experience in Italy*. Routledge, 1998.

■ Ridley, Jaspar. *Mussolini*. St. Martin's Press, 1998.

■ Spackman, Barbara. *Fascist Virilities: Rhetoric, Ideology and Social Fantasy in Italy*. University of Minnesota, 1996.

■ Stille, Alexander. *Benevolence and Betrayal: Five Italian Jewish Families under Fascism*. Penguin USA, 1993.

■ Stone, Marla Susan. *The Patron State: Culture and Politics in Fascist Italy*. Princeton University Press, 1999.

■ Whittam, John. *Fascist Italy*. Manchester University Press, 1995.

1919 On March 23, Mussolini founds the *fasci di combattimento* in Milan.

1921 In the May elections, the fascists elect 35 deputies. By November, the movement has transformed itself into the *Partito Nazionale Fascista* (PNF, National Fascist Party).

1922 In May, the PNF organizes over 300,000 members. On October 29, after the fascist march on Rome, King Victor Emmanuel III charges Mussolini with forming a new government.

1923 The Fascist Grand Council and the volunteer militia for national security are organized. The Nationalist Party merges with the National Fascist Party. A new majority electoral law is passed.

1924 In the April elections, the list of fascists and their allies wins over 60% of the vote. In June Socialist deputy Giacomo Matteotti is kidnapped and assassinated.

1925 The new law on the powers of the head of the government is ratified. *Confindustria* and the fascist unions sign the Vidoni Palace Pact. The National After-Work recreational project is created.

1926 New laws are passed on the executive's power to establish legal norms, the decline of antifascist deputies, the abolition of communal council elections, and the abolition of the freedom of the press and political/union association. A new public security law is passed. The Special Tribunal is formed and the death penalty reintroduced. The National Balilla is formed.

1928 The so-called "constitutionalization" of the Grand Council takes place.

1929 February 11: the Lateran Pacts are jointly signed by the Catholic Church and the Fascist State.

1932 The National Fascist Party reopens registration, and sets off on a path to reach a membership of over 1,500,000.

1934 Mussolini issues first orders to his military chiefs regarding the conquest of Ethiopia.

1935 In October, the Italian army attacks Ethiopia. In November, the League of Nations proclaims economic sanctions against Italy.

1936 In May, with the conquest of Ethiopia complete, the Empire is proclaimed. In July, General Franco of Spain receives the first installment of aid from the fascists. The Spanish Civil War begins. In October, the Rome-Berlin Axis is formed.

1937 Italy abandons the League of Nations.

1938 The racial laws are introduced in Italy. The Munich Agreement fails to impede the partitioning of Czechoslovakia.

1939 In April, Italy annexes Albania. In May, Italy and Germany sign the Pact of Steel. In September, at the outbreak of the world war, Italy declares herself to be a non-belligerent.

1940 On June 10, Italy enters the war against France and England. In October, Mussolini launches an attack against Greece.

1941 Mussolini stands by Hitler in the attack against the Soviet Union. Yugoslavia is militarily occupied by Italian and German troops. Japan, Italy and Germany enter into war against the United States. The Italians suffer a series of military defeats in Africa. The first allied aerial bombardments on Italian soil.

1943 In March, workers' strikes are organized in Turin and Milan. In July, the Allies occupy Sicily. During the night of July 24th, the Grand Council reduces Mussolini's rank, the king forces him to resign and places him under arrest. Badoglio is named head of the government. On September 8, Italy signs the armistice, but the Germans, with a blitz on the Gran Sasso, free *Il Duce* and occupy those regions of Italy not yet under Allied control. Between September and October, in North-Central Italy, the Italian Social Republic is formed — a Fascist state guided by Mussolini under German protection.

1944 The Allies advance toward the north: Rome and Tuscany are liberated.

1945 In April, the Resistance orders a general insurrection: the country is liberated by the partisans and by American and British forces. Mussolini is executed near Dongo.

Index of names

The Traveller's History Series